GIRL

FROM THE

SOUTHSIDE

A Life and Times in the Art of Ballet

DOROTHY PERCIVAL

A Biography by D. Joseph Benson

Table of Contents

Preface   1

Chapter 1: Early Life and Discovering Ballet   5

Chapter 2: Working for Elva and Starting her Own Studio   12

Chapter 3: Meeting Margret Smallie   16

Chapter 4: Meeting Jim   19

Chapter 5: The Troubles of Family Life   23

Chapter 6: Ballet San Joaquin Gets its Own Studio   26

Chapter 7: Practicing with the San Francisco Ballet & Sacramento Ballet   31

Chapter 8: Voices of the Students   34

Chapter 9: A Complex Relationship   46

Chapter 10: Pushing Her Students   52

Chapter 11: Dorothy Goes to College   70

Chapter 12: Meeting Norbet Vesak   78

Chapter 13: Doing work for the San Francisco Opera Ballet   84

Chapter 14: Passing of Loved Ones   87

Photo Gallery   90

Chapter 15: Working with Joffrey Ballet   97

Chapter 16: Dorothy's Rigorous Encouragement   102

Chapter 17: Cold War Era Ballet   106

Chapter 18: Charter member of the Pacific Northwest Regional Ballet Association   110

Chapter 19: Departing from Dorothy   128

Chapter 20: A Mother/ Daughter team   131

Chapter 21: Awards and Losses   133

Chapter 22: Dorothy "The Bitch" Percival   140

Chapter 23: The Nutcracker   155

Chapter 24: Crossing Paths With Dorothy   162

Chapter 25: Loss of the Stockton Studio   168

Chapter 26: The COVID-19 Pandemic   170

Chapter 27: Dorothy's Impact on her Students   172

Chapter 28: Dorothy on the art of teaching ballet   189

Epilogue   192

End Pages   195

PREFACE

When it comes to artists, we often look merely at the finished result and get nothing more than a glance at the process that leads up to it. We, as the ballet audience, really have no way of knowing the journey that took place in order to get everyone to that stage. Ballet choreographer Dorothy Percival has been through that journey so many times that she could do it in her sleep. The fluid motions of ballet are muscle memory to her— the hours and hours of practicing the same positions and poses over and over again have shaped her literally and figuratively into who she is today.

I first met Dorothy when I was probably around 15 years old. My mother began bringing my sister to her for ballet lessons at Dorothy's studio in Stockton, California. For years, I spent time going to her shows, watching the work that the dancers put in on stage in order to live up to Dorothy's standards of perfection. As a teenage boy who never really cared about ballet, I began to appreciate it because it became impossible not to. As I got older, I began taking my sister to ballet rehearsals and sitting for hours in the waiting room doing homework. The waiting room in Dorothy's studio was full of antique furniture and pictures of her ballet glory days. While sitting in there, you could hear the thud of dancers bouncing across the studio floor upstairs and

Dorothy barking corrections. You could hear the work going into getting every single position perfect.

Dorothy had been floating around the idea that she wanted to have her life and career documented in a book for years. She had mentioned this over the phone to my mother, Lisa, who promptly said, "Danny will do it!" without even asking me. Who needs an agent when you have your mom? I was initially very hesitant as I was still a senior in college who was used to writing cheesy sci-fi stories, and my only non-fiction work was blogs and articles about cars. Ballet was something I knew little to nothing about outside of watching Dorothy's shows. But I just couldn't say no to someone like Dorothy. So, I decided to schedule a meeting with her at her home in Lodi, California.

By this point, she was 89 years old, which means there was a lot to cover in this book. Her house is situated on a street corner surrounded by cornfields with very few neighbors. As I pulled up in my car, I couldn't even see her house as her property was covered by very tall cypress trees. I parked on the side of the road and opened up the gate to her front yard, which was immaculate. The grass was perfectly green with a stone pathway that snaked through it with trees scattered throughout. As I made my way to the porch, windchimes made their music in the breeze. I looked around at her potted plants, the paint peeling off of the wooden deck, and the two folding directors' chairs she had next to the front door. It all made me feel a little more at ease as I took a breath and knocked on the door. As soon as I knocked, her chihuahua, Tiny Tina, began to bark. Dorothy opened the door. She had long, dark, greying hair, and even at

89 years old, she still carried herself like someone in the prime of her life, still maintaining her dancer's physique.

As I stepped into her house, it was like stepping into another world, Dorothy's world. Her house, which used to be Lodi's community center in the early 1900s, looks like a theater combined with a museum. She wanted to start out by giving me a tour; she first showed me the living room, which used to be a stage, a place that Dorothy is very used to being. Just below the living room is a sitting area near a fireplace, one of two in the house; both spaces are full of antique furniture and collectibles. She showed me her glass elephant collection; she must have close to 100 in the house. She very proudly showed me the first one she ever got at the Golden Gate International Exposition in San Francisco in 1939. Among her many other collectibles, which included sculptures and paintings, the things that stuck out the most were posters and pictures of her long career in ballet. Beautiful black and white pictures of herself and her students that so eloquently captured the elegance of ballet. Then there were the dozens of posters displayed throughout her home; some of the posters were created for Dorothy's shows, and others were advertising ballets of Dorothy's many close friends. The art in the posters conveyed just enough mystery to get you to watch the various performances put on by Dorothy and other artistic directors. My favorite rooms, however, were her basement and her library. Her basement is full of trunks upon trunks filled with clothes and props from her numerous shows over the years. Many of the costumes she made. As she opened up the trunks, I picked up some of the costumes, and I could picture the dancers on stage, bringing life to the tulle and sequined materials I held in my hands. The sheer number of trunks that lined the wall and stacked up the ceiling showed me just how long Dorothy's career in ballet had been. We then made our way to the library, which was full of shelves packed with books and VHS tapes with titles of her earlier shows written on masking tape. The shelves were only broken up by more pictures of her students— it was truly a room where you could get lost in the history, with books upon books about ballet history, techniques, and choreographers much like herself. Dorothy moved throughout her house like she was in ballet, not wasting any movement, so fluent and eloquent. She picked up Tiny Tina and led me back to the sitting area around the fireplace. I sat on the brown leather couch, and she sat in her rocking chair with Tiny Tina in her lap, very eager to tell her story. After seeing her house, I felt like I understood her a lot more, which made getting her story feel much less daunting. So I pulled out my phone and hit the audio recording button. Dorothy took me back to the beginning: Tracy, California, 1930.

The Early Years:
1930-Late 50's

CHAPTER 1

Early Life and Discovering Ballet

Dorothy Percival was born Dorothy Gebhardt on August 29th, 1930 to Walter and Mary Bessy Percival in the small dusty farm town of Tracy, located in the San Joaquin Valley of California. Dorothy was named after a close friend whom her mother looked up to when she was younger. The Percivals lived on the southside of Tracy during the Depression era, when times were, of course, very hard. Her father was of European descent and worked for the railroad moving carts, loading and unloading trains for ten cents an hour. Dorothy really admired her father and described him as "the nicest man in the world: everybody liked Dad."

Her mother was half Mexican and half Native American. Of her, Dorothy explained, "She was adorable number one, always there, always good to me, tried to keep me on the straight and narrow without pushing her ideas on me. And she was beautiful with black hair, just a pretty girl. She was not a demanding mother except that I had to keep my room clean and I had to be respectful. She is probably one of the kindest people without being sloppy. Her heart was kind and she knew she had a child that was going to be somebody. She was kind of a performer." Dorothy's family history runs back a long time in California, with her maternal Great Grandfather being one of the state rangers tasked with capturing the real-life Robin Hood-type outlaw Joaquin Murrieta. But her grandfather refused to do so since Murrieta was robbing from the rich and giving to the poor, a decision that cost him his badge. An old black and white photo of him sitting in a chair wearing a suit can be seen in her house hanging above her piano.

Before she was in school, around the age of four or five, Dorothy would wait for her father to come home every day for lunch and ask her mother "When's Daddy coming home?" to which Mary Bessy would always respond "Pretty soon." Dorothy would ask this over and over again, as she was always so excited to see her father. She had three older sisters, Marieta, Ruby, and Billy who were all in school; meaning that Dorothy was home alone with her mother all day.

"I think probably I wasn't the favorite child, I think my sister two years older than me was. She had lots of talent, she was kind of a performer because of our Mexican and Indian background. My grandfather Renaldo Gallego was my first dance partner. Dancing was a big thing in the family although my grandfather and grandmother had been divorced for many years."

Dancing and performing have always been a big part of Dorothy's family, going all the way back to her grandparents on her mothers' side. She described her childhood home as having a long driveway that was connected to the main road. There was a garage on the side, one side for the car and the other side for a shop. She would wait in front of the garage door in anticipation when she would see her father coming down the road. She would dash down the dusty dirt road and meet him at the end of the driveway where he would throw her up in the air and put her on his shoulders.

The southside of Tracy where Dorothy grew up was the poorer part of town, where the people affected most by the Depression lived. Filled with people of different ethnic and cultural backgrounds, Dorothy describes her neighborhood as a "melting pot." She said there was a Mexican family who lived across the street, with a whole group of kids who were all being raised by a single mother. Many suspected that the mother was "running a house" to make ends meet. Dorothy describes her neighborhood as also having a lot of Portuguese people as well as a few Irish and Italian families. She distinctly remembers the father of one of the Italian families having a very snobbish attitude and thinking he was better than everyone else.

At this time Dorothy said that for some reason she wanted a baby doll that was African American, despite the fact that she had yet to meet a Black person. Her parents told her that they don't make baby dolls that are Black, so for Christmas, they bought her a baby doll that was white. Dorothy thought this was one of the ugliest things she had ever seen and absolutely hated it. She hated it so much that she would throw it down the stairs of her house because "It was too ugly." Later on, a Black family moved into the neighborhood and Dorothy had become friends with their daughter, Juanita. Dorothy loved to visit

Juanita's home because it was a railroad boxcar that had been converted over to a house.

Another childhood friend that Dorothy fondly remembers was a Chinese girl named May-Lee whose parents owned a bar. She remembers entering the bar to look for May-Lee, and seeing the various men at the bar turning around in surprise upon seeing a little girl come in through the tall doors. May-Lee's father quickly ushered Dorothy to their apartment building behind the bar.

Dorothy's mother was the interpreter for everyone in the neighborhood, mainly for the Italian and Portuguese families because she could understand them. The different cultures were a big part of Dorothy's childhood, from her neighbors to her mother making homemade Mexican meals.

Dorothy was raised in a Christian household. Though religion has always been a part of her life, she explained, "If you listen closely I'm not what you call a church-going person. I was raised Church of Christ. My mother was Catholic but when she married dad she changed. In the summers, I would go to this event they would have for kids, and it was [run by] Baptists." Dorothy explained how she still had one of the craft projects that she had made as a child during these events: a sock that she made which she still has hanging up in her bedroom.

"If you believe that there is a supreme being, I have a little problem with people who always say it's Jehova, Latter-Day Saints, Catholic, Baptists, Methodists, Presbyterian. It's all the same being you know? Don't tell me your religion is better than this religion— and you would have to go a long, long way in any religion to find two people like my mother and father who matched with kindness and understanding."

Dorothy describes never being forced when it came to religion in her family, but that she would always attend church with them. The people at her church were always kind and welcoming. She remembered a person named Mr. Russel, a giant of a man who would always have candy for Dorothy in the front pocket of his jacket. "...and that was the Church of Christ, wonderful man [Mr. Russel] and wonderful people."

When Dorothy was nine years old, her neighbor who was the same age, from a Portuguese family, asked Dorothy if she was going to take dancing lessons.

Dorothy asked, "What are dancing lessons?"

Her neighbor said, "You know sometimes when you get to go to the movies and they play music and people jump around?"

Dorothy said, "Yeah I like to jump around to music."

But when she asked her parents, she found out that they were ten cents a lesson at the Odd Fellows Hall in Tracy across from the Western Pacific Railroad tracks, and her father said, "Oh hun, ten cents a lesson is two loaves of bread and two quarts of milk." Dorothy's famous persistent and vocal personality clearly started at a young age, because she was able to convince her parents to sign her up for lessons.

Elva Eilers was Dorothy's first ballet instructor who was traveling around San Joaquin Valley giving lessons. Dorothy was a poor southside girl who didn't have much— not seeing much outside of going to the movie theater once in a while so walking through the giant doors of the hall was a big experience for her. She described the building as very tall, with doors at the end of the front hallway that lead to a ballroom. "I thought I had died and gone to heaven right then." said Dorothy as she entered the ballroom.

When she first saw Elva, she was dressed in a black leotard, black chiffon skirt, pink tights, and pink ballet shoes. Dorothy described her as "The angel in heaven." That was it. Dorothy took her first lesson and said she would never quit, "It was the best experience and has always been the best experience."

CHAPTER 2

Working for Elva and Starting her Own Studio

D orothy continued dancing throughout her childhood and into her teenage years. Times began to get better in the United States, as it slowly pulled itself out of the Great Depression. When she could, Mary Bessy would drive Dorothy from Tracy to Stockton to continue with lessons from Elva, otherwise Dorothy would take the bus. Her mother was very supportive of her during this time. "The moment I decided what I wanted to be there was no controversy, it was what I wanted to be, where I wanted to go, what I wanted to do. She made all of my costumes, was real proud of what I did, and helped with everything. I probably had the best mother ever and I never wanted to disappoint her. And I didn't, just being who I was and being respectful. I didn't have to expect her to have to make my costumes or to take me to practice, it was always a pleasure for her to do it. I learned from her a sense of calmness but also not to take any baloney, don't let people walk all over you."

An interesting note that Dorothy mentioned is the fact that she sensed that her mother always wanted to be a career woman, which is a trait that she must have inherited from her as she started hosting her own dance lessons at the age of fifteen under her teacher Elva.

Dorothy didn't know a lot about Elva's personal life outside of her just being a dance teacher.

"She worked during the Depression times, she traveled to different towns: one was Tracy, one was Livermore, and the other was I think Manteca. Each one day a week because she had to eat. And I think she was a Mormon because she came from Utah, I think her family was Mormon. And she was strict, I was her pet, I became her pet right away because I like to dance and I wanted to do it."

Dorothy would rent out her own space in Elva's Tracy studio and pay her own bills from the revenue she would get from her students. During this time Dorothy began to become more independent when it came to dancing, finding ways for her to balance her life and education.

Eventually, Dorothy had to figure out how to get to and from Tracy to Stockton in order to attend Elva's dance lessons every week. She knew that the bus would pass by her high school every day around noon. Being the determined person she is, Dorothy went to the bus station and asked "Would you please have them stop for me at the school? I'll be waiting out front for them exactly when they stop by." Dorothy knew from a young age you had to be persistent to get to where you want to be: "Do it in a nice way, but if it can't be done in a nice way, do it whatever way you have to."

The teller at the station said no, but Dorothy wouldn't give up.

"Aw come on, I have to get to Stockton and this is the only way! I promise I'll be there. He won't even have to stop for me, he can slow down, open the door and I'll jump on!"

The Teller told Dorothy to hang on and went to the back. She came out looking surprised and said, "They're going to stop for you."

The elated Dorothy responded with "Of course they will stop for me!"

The next thing Dorothy had to deal with was explaining this situation to her history teacher, Mr. Moore. In her history class the next day, Mr. Moore was pacing up and down the rows of students.

When he walked past her desk she asked "Mr. Moore, can I please get out of class at 11:30 on Fridays?"

He asked why and Dorothy explained, "I have to catch a bus, they're going to stop for me in front of the school and I have to get to Stockton."

"Dorothy I can't do that, I can't let you out like that." said Mr. Moore.

Dorothy pleaded with her teacher, "But Mr. Moore I've got to." But Mr. Moore repeated that he couldn't do that. Dorothy put her head down on her desk and began to cry thinking of how she was going to explain to her parents that she had to quit school in order to pursue dancing.

Later that week, while sitting at her desk she felt a tap on her shoulder from Mr. Moore.

Dorothy looked up and Mr. Moore said "Dorothy, it seems as if I pass by your desk every Friday around 11:00, and you happen

to be gone when I turn back around, I wouldn't even remember
if you were there in the first place."

He was going to let her go, and Dorothy was elated. Every
Friday he would give her a wink and turn a blind eye to Dorothy bolting out the door to catch her bus. Dorothy credits Mr.
Moore a lot, saying "Without Mr. Moore, I would have never
been able to graduate high school."

By her senior year, Dorothy found that by teaching her own
ballet classes in Tracy, attending high school, and taking lessons
from Elva, she was having a difficult time balancing all three.
So Dorothy eventually came to the decision that she had to stop
attending Elva's classes.

"Except when I got to be older and had to work on my own,
she was concerned because I wasn't running back and forth to
Stockton anymore because I had my own studio in Tracy and
I couldn't run back and forth. She became a little bit undercut,
at least that's what I thought. And as I've gotten older I thought
I probably hurt her feelings, you know? I probably did because
I quit and didn't come back to visit her because I was going
everywhere else. As I got older I thought about it more, I don't
think she realized the importance she was in my life. To intro-
duce me to the dance and make me like it so much that I went
further. I was really darn fortunate. If you believe that a supreme being gave you a gift, why are you going to screw it up?"

Dorothy eventually graduated high school in the mid 1940s.
When asked about her high school experience, Dorothy said
"It just didn't mean anything to me, there was nothing there I
could use. I mean I already knew how to read and write. I could
add and subtract. That's as far as I figured I had to go."

CHAPTER 3

Meeting Margret Smallie

In the 1940s, a lifelong friend came into Dorothy's life. When she began forming connections with other teachers in the dance community around the San Joaquin Valley, Dorothy came into contact with a woman named Margret Smallie. "I had my classes, and she heard about my classes. And I was always willing to talk to any dance teacher around. I was beginning to think about the studio, a company a long time. So I've gotten in touch with a lot of the teachers in the town, and she was one of them. Would you think about getting together and starting a company sort of thing? She was one of the only ones: the rest of them would come in if they thought they gain to get something out of it monetarily."

As Dorothy explained more about Margret's teaching methods to me, the differences between their two teaching styles became very evident. It also became clear to me how so many ballet instructors differ with their approaches to teaching the art of ballet. Dorothy attributed Margret's style of teaching/dancing to where she grew up:

"Margret was born, raised, and trained in Germany. And you didn't really have much to say about anything there, so everything was right smack dab how the instructors were where they were."

It is worth noting that at the age of seven Margret's life was turned on its head when the Nazis had taken over Germany, leading to her being separated from her family and eventually reuniting with them in the United States.

Dorothy continued, "As I understood it, the teachers and the government were just 'This is how we do it and how it's done no question.' She was a product of that Cecchetti style."

The Cecchetti method is a form of ballet in which no move is wasted, every move has a point to serve the overall ballet. It was first introduced by Maestro Enrico Cecchetti in the 19th-century. The Cecchetti Council of America defines the Cecchetti style as, "Cecchetti training is a rigorous method which pays careful attention to the laws of anatomy. It develops all of the qualities essential to the dancer: balance, poise, strength, elevation, elasticity, 'ballon,' etc. It is classic in its purity and clear-cut style."

Dorothy continued, "It was their way period, how the teacher presented it, how they're supposed to present it, and how they did present it. Rather than saying, 'Okay, let's get at it from a different direction, we'll get the same thing accomplished.' So the book in Cecchetti says 'This is what is done you better not do it differently, or better not get the same outcome with a different approach.' Because everybody's different, you're different than me, or I'm different than my family— but our outcome has to be the same. How you go get it is the material actually— and each person that is going to the classes and searching for that outcome are different too. Each individual has to be taught individually the same stuff that you're teaching everybody."

Dorothy was pretty critical of the ways that Margret was taught ballet, as she felt that it really shut the door on creativity for the students. "There was no expansion or nothing that came from the heart or from the mind." she said. However, despite her disagreements with this style, she still very much respected Margret as a teacher.

"I think that she appreciated my approach. I appreciated the knowledge that she had, I didn't appreciate how she got it because the students were very automatic rather than letting them flow into it. The outcome was the same except when you saw it on stage, that type of training is brutal on stage and technically perfect."

Dorothy's theory (as to what drew them together) is that her teaching style allowed her to break away from the traditional Cecchetti style. "I think what she saw in me was freedom. Freedom to express herself emotionally, as well as verbally."

Margret and Dorothy's partnership eventually evolved into a friendship. And even after Margret went on to start her own school, she still worked with Dorothy frequently, even sending some of her students to Dorothy's ballet company when she felt that they were ready.

CHAPTER 4

Meeting Jim

On a hot summer's day in the late 1940s , Dorothy had decided to take a day off from ballet to go to a local pool with her friend. As she was sunbathing on the side of the pool she heard a voice from behind her say "I wonder what it looks like standing up?"

Dorothy chuckled, "I had no idea what he was talking about so I turned over and there were two boys. One was a tall blonde-haired boy and the other was a tall dark-haired boy. So we talked and the blonde-haired boy asked me out which ended up making the dark-haired boy, Jim, upset. I ended up going out with that kid but I didn't like him, he was too full of himself. Plus by this time I was busy dancing, teaching, and running around. But then Jim asked me out. It turns out he was the one who said 'I wonder what it looks like standing up?' I thought the blonde boy was more to my tastes but he wasn't, he was a jerk."

Jim and Dorothy began dating, and eventually got married in 1949. As Dorothy puts it, "As soon as we started going out we knew that we were going to be together."

She describes Jim as "Complicated. As I got older I understood it more. He was really talented, loved baseball. He could have, if he had the proper parents, been a professional baseball player. He was always trying to prove himself: although he was extremely intelligent, [he] couldn't do what he wanted to do because he needed backing from his parents."

Dorothy knew Jim had an appreciation for the arts because as her school expanded, she began putting on performances. Jim was the one building the sets, which showed his immense craftsmanship when it came to carpentry, lighting, and painting.

"He did the lighting, he did the scenery, everything. Because he was so smart, and it kind of took care of the disappointment he had because he could've done anything had he had smart parents. He was handsome and very, very caring, protective in a gruff way."

Jim really embraced Dorothy's career and was always there when she needed it, something that was not very common for husbands and wives at the time. There were certain expectations of what women should be during this time period, and it certainly was not very common for a woman to be a career individual back then. Nor was it common for a man to want to express himself through the arts. But Dorothy and Jim's relationship defied how most of society in the United States thought the stereotypical nuclear family should be in the 1950s. A funny example of this was Dorothy's disdain for cooking. She described how her mother would cook all kinds of great food, but it was just something Dorothy never liked to do. So Jim

picked up that part of that relationship because as Dorothy described it, "He had to or else the poor man would have starved."
As much as Dorothy and Jim had a strong relationship and
got along well, the same could not be said for the relationship
between Dorothy and Jim's parents.

"He was an artist and nobody really knew about it." said Dorothy as she pointed to one of Jim's many beautiful oil paintings
she had displayed throughout her house.

"He was an artist, he was an athlete with a jerk mother and
an alcoholic father. His mother was a pain in the ass, she had
an attitude."

Dorothy explained how Jim had done an oil painting as a
gift for his parents and when he gave it to them his father
insulted him.

"What, do you sit to pee now Jim?" Jim's father said when he
received the painting.

Dorothy snatched the painting out of her father-in- law's hands
and said he didn't deserve it. Dorothy and her relationship with
her in-laws was always rocky and eventually, it came to a head:

"We were going to get a new car, a new Ford. And Jim said he
had to bring his mother along and I said no. 'If you take your
mother along, we don't get a new car.'"

"Oh you're terrible," said Jim.

"Yeah, I know. but it's my car, not hers," said Dorothy.

She didn't like me very much either, but anyways we got the
new car, a blueish-green color. Brand new car that, of course,
my business was helping to pay for."

At the time, Jim was working for the California Water Service and they lived in pretty much a shack. After they had picked up the new car Dorothy said to Jim:

"Let's go down and show your mom the new car."

"You're terrible," Jim said once again.

"Yeah, I know," chuckled Dorothy.

Dorothy had to put her foot down at this point in their relationship. According to her, "Either you're going to go to bed with Mommy or you're going to go to bed with me. Take your pick. So we drove by and Mommy comes up to the door when we pull into the driveway and she says 'Oh Jimmy I didn't know you were going to get a new car.'

"And I said, 'You didn't? Jim how terrible of you not to tell your mother.'"

Dorothy began laughing and said "I think that's the last time I ever spoke to her. She was screwing around with me, a southside Tracy girl. I didn't like her, I never liked her. To this day I still don't, she always just thought she was hot stuff."

CHAPTER 5

The Troubles of Family Life

Dorothy was hyperfocused on her career and still young. Nothing could take Dorothy's focus away from her art, except becoming a mom.

Dorothy became pregnant with her first daughter Tamara, and gave birth to her on August 17, 1950. Around the same time Tamara was born, Dorothy and Jim were having relationship problems. This led to the couple separating and Dorothy living in her own apartment when Tamara was born. The new parents decided that Dorothy would have the baby during the week, and Jim would take his daughter on the weekends. It was not an ideal situation.

One day, Dorothy's parents – Walter and Mary Bessy– were visiting Dorothy when Jim came over to pick up Tamara. The details are fuzzy for Dorothy for this specific incident but she does not remember the meeting to be pleasant. But one thing that vividly stuck out to Dorothy was her father's reaction to Dorothy's and Jim's living arrangement. As she recalls, her father began to cry about Tamara being taken away from her mother for days at a time, especially with her still being a baby.

He pleaded with Jim to leave the baby with Dorothy stating, "A mother shouldn't be separated from her child like that." Walter talked with the separated couple leading to Dorothy and Jim working things out, and eventually moving back in together. Dorothy had mentioned this as an example of how loving and caring of a person her father was.

A couple of years later, Dorothy became pregnant with her second daughter Kimberli. On Febuary 14, 1952, Kimberli was born. All of this meant that she had to be at home in the mid-day raising her family, until Jim got home from work later in the day. And while Dorothy loved being a mom, she was beginning to go stir crazy and had become lonely. Of the thought of being a housewife, Dorothy had this to say: "Having babies is okay, but especially when you have another part of your life that was given to you by a higher being it's hard to make them understand that I love you [her loved ones] a lot but I also love this [craft]. It's a balance. And you're going to go off and marry who you want to and I'm going to be at home going crazy because I didn't get to do what I did?"

Seeing how a forced retirement is driving Dorothy crazy right now as I write this makes me wonder how much it was driving her crazy when she was young. And what Dorothy had said about trying to show that "...I love you a lot but I also love this." is something that I think all artists whose lives revolve around their art struggle with. Since Dorothy was so busy balancing motherhood and her job as a ballet instructor, she didn't have much time to make friends outside of dance, except for one. "After I had children and everything, I had two women come to my door, one was a young woman. I was home, I was going cra-

zy just like I am now, maybe a little worse because I was younger. And there was a knock on the door and this young woman
[appeared], probably a little bit younger than I was at the time, I
was about twenty."

The women at the door were Jehovah's Witnesses, and the
younger woman was named Josephine Eliot. Dorothy invited
Josephine in to talk.

"Anyways she came in and I said, 'Could you come once a week
and talk to me?'"

Josephine said, "Oh I'm just here to give you this magazine."
Dorothy responded with, "Oh then you have to leave."

Josephine ended up leaving, but just a few days later there was
another knock on the door. Josephine had decided to come
back. "In her arm was an 'Awake Magazine.' I knew that she was
a Jehovah's Witness and I said "You've come just in time." She
almost fell off the porch because they're not used to being treated like that. So she came in and I asked her again if she could
come once a week. She said yes she could. And she gave me a
lesson, we just got together."

CHAPTER 6

Ballet San Joaquin Gets its Own Studio

Dorothy's company, which she named Ballet San Joaquin, did not have a permanent home until the late 1950s. She had been renting out school auditoriums and such, but with two children and finally having enough money, Dorothy and Jim finally purchased a home in Stockton, California. This was not just going to be a home for the family though, this was also going to be a home for Ballet San Joaquin. Jim and Dorothy began renovating the house to include a full upstairs ballet studio: complete with a downstairs waiting room, and separate living quarters for the family. Finally, Ballet San Joaquin had its own studio.

As Tamara and Kimberli grew, they inevitably began practicing ballet under their mother right in the home studio. But Dorothy soon figured out that being mother and teacher to your children at the same time would be far more complicated than it looked. "Well Tamara was very talented, so was Kimberli. But being a mother who was a disciplinarian at home and in the theater made it difficult for them to accept me as a mom."

I could tell that this was a difficult subject for Dorothy to talk about, as this situation with Tamara and Kimberli is just as complicated today as it was back then.

"Do you think they saw you as a coach all the time?" I asked.

"Pretty much." Dorothy replied.

I could very much tell by her response that she wanted to move on to a different subject. So I decided to go to the next two people on the other side of this...

TAMARA WAGNER *is Dorothy's first daughter.*

My name is Tamara Wagner.

KIMBERLI CAMPBELL *is Dorothy's second daughter.*

My name is Kimberli Campbell and my maiden name is Kimberli Dephart.

TAMARA WAGNER

[My mother] was really into her art form and spent a lot of time at that, and that took a lot of her time. She was strict, but she gave me a really good background in classical ballet and demanded proper behavior in the classroom. Which was good, it taught me a lot about accomplishing things, getting from the beginning of something to the end of something with all the production and all of that. The expectations of the people who were in the productions that relied on me. And that was all good but as a teenager, of course, I wasn't real wild about it but I learned a lot of good things.

KIMBERLI CAMPBELL

It was an interesting relationship having a dual-parent, as a parent and a professional. As a person, you sort of evolve into your understanding of relationships and everything that went on in your life when you look back. A lot of opportunities came from her quest, and from that a lot of interesting twists and turns in our personal life. But she's an admirable person that's for sure. When you're growing up anything you live with is normal but as you grow older you view things a bit differently or understand them a little differently. Our life was always the way it was that my mom was a constant professional and dedicated to her passion of dance and that's just how we kind of grew up.

It was kind of a nontraditional family setting, I think when I look back on it for the '50s and '60s. My father was more of the homebody person and my mother was out as a professional and striving for her passion. When we were growing up you don't question how things are and then when you get older and think back you realize my life wasn't like anyone else's lives that I knew. So that was interesting, you know when I look back on it as an adult but growing up it was a normal state of affairs. My father was the grocery shopper, the ironer, and the laundry guy— he cooked the meals and did all that stuff. In that era it was a little more unusual I think.

I think [ballet] instilled a very intense respect for discipline. There wasn't a lot of room to mess around because classical ballet is a pretty strict discipline in itself.

I think it was a little whirl of a trio, kind of a three musketeers thing in our house. My mother had her passion with ballet and we, her daughters, were kind of brought along into it. So that was kind of a world unto itself, and when I think back on it every year we would go some place with my mom on a vacation: we went to Disneyland, we went to Laguna Beach, we went to Carmel. We did different things like that but just with my mother, and I think that was really important to her to have specific time not revolving around the dance studio. We would drive away and my dad would always stay home which I thought was always a bit unusual. Like I said, our life was unusual but I really didn't question it then. But when I look back on it I think that's probably why she wanted that moment with us only. Because she was so absorbed with her goals which took a lot of her time and attention.

I think it was a very non-traditional family. And I don't know whether that was a negative where it really took away from us. It was just very non-traditional. So I think if you're viewing it from a very traditional aspect the answer to that question would be yes, but not necessarily in a negative way. Because it was a norm at that time for me, for my personality and how I evolved through the whole thing.

When [Dorothy] could be silly she would be really, really silly. And I remember those kinds of funny things, I don't know. But every once in a while you catch people at the right times where everything is just right and they're just really silly. I can remember her pretending that she was some kind of a monster and chasing us around and crawling after us like a little monster. I don't even know how to describe it, it was just funny. Then she always came in and kissed goodnight in bed for years, that was a very tender thing. We would go to bed and call for Mom and she would come in and kiss us goodnight and tuck us into bed.

I noticed sometimes that that doesn't happen for kids anymore. And then just going off on adventures where she wanted to go, it was always kind of interesting. We spent a summer in Carmel one time and that's very strong in my mind, I was maybe ten. My dad would come over on the weekends and stay there with us, and we'd stay there with her while she was doing musical theater. And then just traveling about, looking back it was a lucky childhood in a lot of ways but complex.

CHAPTER 7

Practicing with the San Francisco
Ballet & Sacramento Ballet

Around the time that Ballet San Joaquin was officially established, Dorothy also began to practice with the San Francisco Ballet. She describes her time there as "Pretty interesting." Dorothy's oldest sister Marietta would sometimes join her when she would go to San Francisco. "Marietta liked the guys and Marietta liked to drink, she was an alcoholic. But she had a beautiful singing voice."

Dorothy explained how they would call Marietta the female Mel Torme. She thought each one of her sisters had a ton of talent, but never really did anything with it. "Maybe it was the times," said Dorothy.

Dorothy began reminiscing about how talented her sisters really were. "Ruby was an artist, I have things that she made for me, see those two figurines?" Dorothy pointed at two sculptures sitting on her shelf.

"She made those?" I asked.

"She made a whole bunch of them and I got three of them. Billy could pick up any instrument and within a short time be able to play it. She played the piano by ear, she played the violin, the

piccolo, the flute. She could pick up in a short time and be able
to play something. All that talent in the family. I don't know
why nobody did anything with it, because I wasn't kept from
doing it."

Dorothy chuckled as she recalled one of the times Marietta
accompanied her to San Francisco. Marietta suggested that the
pair should go get lunch before Dorothy went to her rehearsal.
Marietta would always have a beer or two while they had lunch,
and Dorothy decided one day that she would have one as well.
During her time with the San Francisco Ballet, Dorothy's
instructor was Harold Christensen, a rather well-known name
in the ballet community. Christensen was the instructor for
the advanced classes at the company. He, along with his two
brothers Lew and William, are credited by many in the ballet
community for introducing the art of ballet to the United States.
Specifically, the West Coast as they founded the San Francisco
Ballet. This makes Dorothy's story even funnier because she
describes Christensen as a "total jackass" who would single her
out because as Dorothy puts it, "she was better than him."

To try and avoid Christensen's wrath, Dorothy would try to
hide towards the back of the class in order to make it harder for
Christensen to find her. On the specific day that Dorothy had
a beer at lunch time with her sister, Christensen did his usual
routine of trying to single Dorothy out, she continued to move
around the back trying to avoid his glare. "I was usually nicer in
class but one beer just does it to me, so I don't drink at all."
Christensen then addressed what Dorothy thought was the
whole class, "What comes forward first in a battement tendu,
the heel or the toe?"

Dorothy paid him no mind as she thought he was addressing
the class and not her.

But Christensen then pointed at Dorothy, "You, what goes first
in the battement tendu?"

Dorothy, with a beer in her system became as defiant
as ever, and responded with "Why the heel, of course,
didn't you know?"

Dorothy accomplished her mission of getting under Christensen's skin because he was livid. Dorothy said that she never
took his class again after this incident because he was a jerk.

Despite her dislike for Harold Christensen, Dorothy continued
to dance with the San Francisco Ballet. But this became harder
as she was running her own company and raising her children
at the same time— San Francisco was almost a two-hour drive
from her home studio.

An opportunity came knocking when she got a call from the
Sacramento Ballet, which was only an hour away from Ballet
San Joaquin.

"I was working my own ballet company and then [the Sacramento Ballet] wanted me to dance for them, so I danced with
them for about eleven years. They needed somebody to fill in
and my oldest daughter [Tamara] became a member there too.
I was always looking for a place to study and it was closer than
San Francisco. I would go to San Francisco maybe once or twice
a week, and then on the weekends go to Sacramento because I
could get performances in Sacramento."

The Prime Years:
60's through the 80's

CHAPTER 8

Voices of the Students

By the time the 1960s rolled around, Dorothy and her studio were beginning what many consider the prime years. Her business was rapidly expanding as more and more students began to roll in due to Dorothy's reputation of being a top notch instructor. Her flourishing reputation grew in not just Stockton and San Joaquin County, but in the ballet community in general.

From these years came the students that Dorothy kept photographs of throughout her house, and I knew I needed to find them. I needed to know what it was like having Dorothy as an instructor and see what kind of lasting impact she has had on their lives.

I knew that the process of finding these students was going to be difficult as Dorothy couldn't possibly remember how to get ahold of every single one of them. Some have kept in touch with her, some have since lost contact, others Dorothy has had a falling out with for various reasons. The first student I was able to get into contact with was Beth Main who then provided me with the names of several of her classmates. I began searching

Facebook, public records, and even Linkedin to find some of
these people. Some of the phone calls and emails went unan-
swered, a few were angry that I even found them because of bad
blood between them and Dorothy. But the majority were more
than happy to sit down and talk with me and the more people I
found, the more stories began to pour out.

BETH MAIN *was Dorothy's student from 1965 to 1985.*
When I was seven years old I guess I was a pretty uptight kid.
I was the eldest of five. My mom didn't know what to do with
my nervous energy and a friend of hers had a daughter in
ballet class with Dorothy. She recommended that to my mom,
that's how it got started. That was probably 1965, and I went to
Larkspur Lane, I can see, I can smell it. Walking up the little
side path to the gate that goes around to the back of the house.
I grew up there, from the age of seven, by the time I was thirteen I was there seven days a week. And until I left for college
that was my second home and Dorothy a second mother. It
just turns out that I was good enough at it and Dorothy really
committed to my training in the way she committed to all of
us, to each of us. Her commitment is total, I didn't realize how
extraordinary it was at the time. It was hard, she was hard, she
was physical with us in ways she said she can't be anymore.
She had a cane, a black cane and she would use it to mark time
on the floor. One two three four, one two three four, and she
would walk around with it and smack us with it, not in a way
that was hurtful but in a way to correct. She'd put her hands on
your hips, move your leg, or turn you, she was literally hands-
on and unforgiving. "Oh no, you can do better than that!" One

of my memories of working with her was always that I could do
better, it was said though in an aspirational way, not in a critical
break-you-down way. Not at all, somehow we knew as tough
as she was, it was because she saw something in you that you
didn't see in yourself and she was going to bring it out of you.
Or if it didn't come out of you it wasn't going to be because she
didn't try, but I can't stress enough how important it is to note
that it was aspirational not punishing, not critical to belittle but
critical to making you see and strive for better. And I loved it.
Home life was not particularly happy, it was a little chaotic, so
I loved the structure and the discipline of that time with Dorothy and my fellow students and going through that together. I
wanted so much to be good for her and eventually, it came to be
wanting to be good at what I was doing, but it began by wanting
to please her. Because again I didn't feel criticized by her, even
when she screamed at me, she'd throw ashtrays across the room.
Oh my gosh, she was, you know, a firecracker as you'd say. But
you didn't feel stupid, you just felt like she saw something and
you needed to catch up with that vision.

ELIZABETH ARCHER *was Dorothy's student from the*
mid-60s to 1973.
I was twelve when I started and I danced with [Dorothy] all the
way until I was nineteen. I graduated high school in 1972 so it
would have been 1973 when I stopped dancing with Dorothy.
So mid 60's to the early '70s.
Dorothy was like a second mom to me because I spent a lot of
time in the studio every day. At an influential time in my life,
and so working hard as a teenager on dance when you could

be doing a lot of other things was a huge commitment. And how she affected me was just how she taught me so much about detail and technique, commitment, being part of a team, and being part of something greater than yourself. She provided an opportunity for us to explore and express ourselves through an art form.

She just provided a lot of guidance, she was really tough, she was strict and she had her way, you know things had to be her way if you will. It's not really the right words I wanted to say but we followed her vision, and that vision while it was strict accomplished a lot of things. And we were very highly trained young athletes and dancers. So that affected me in a lot of different ways and it's interesting I've given some thought to that. You know when you are a dancer, when you are trained as a dancer you are very detail oriented, highly organized, you anticipate— I use it as an example. When you're learning choreography you have to anticipate what your fellow dancers are doing around you, you have to be open to whatever comes your way, especially from a performer's aspect. You have to be ready to go on stage, you're constantly thinking ahead but you're also really in your body. Ballet especially is such internal work.

[Dorothy] was very welcoming, very supportive, enthusiastic, friendly. There were times, I wouldn't ever say I was afraid of her, but I knew where her lines were. And you know there were times when I was super frustrated with her because she expected so much and she drove us really, really hard. So some of those times especially pre-performance were super emotional because it was like I can't do this one more time, I can't do this step, this sequence, I can't dig deep into my emotional performance one more time.

But I did it, because of her, because she was driving us— the results were phenomenal. Again that has affected so many parts of my life even as an artistic director of my own company and the relationships you have with your own dancers.

You become a nurturing person, and she was a very nurturing person— but she called you to the carpet. You had to be present, you had to be responsible, you had other people relying on you. She was very masterful at bringing that home.

I just couldn't get enough of it, I started late, I didn't even start taking ballet until I was twelve in sixth grade and I ended up going to a ballet class with a friend. From there on out it was my thing, this was what I was meant to do with my life because I was a young athlete, a tomboy in those days. I was always playing soccer and baseball with the boy on the block, but I had a creative imagination that I was able to channel into my dance and it was so rewarding and to this day still is.

"What were the times Dorothy pushed you the most?"
Usually pre-performance when we had a big concert coming up. So I started when I was twelve and by fifteen I was on points, that's a lot of hard work in a three year period of time, it's a huge commitment. So pre-performance, that dedication to the cause if you will, and the perfection of the performance which as we know there is no such thing as perfection. I can't say I was aware of that in those days or at that time. I just knew I had to do my best and I would be really upset if I let my fellow dancers down or I messed up on stage. It's weird processing as a team because when you're so driven that way and you know the

expectation is so high you don't want to let anybody down. It's a place that you really don't fully understand until you become an adult and you're more involved in life and you see that, that's just the way life rolls. You're not going to ever be perfect but it's okay to strive for that, it's a lot of pressure to put on yourself so I would say that I had to learn to let go of some things, to let go of striving to be perfect. It did take a lot of weight off of my shoulders but again as a teenager, you're just driven, you're just doing it, you're in the midst. Those times were tough, when you knew that there was a lot riding on a performance so you just dug deep and you brought forth the best that you could and had to try and live with the result. It was definitely rewarding, some of the most rewarding things I've ever done in my life.

I think from a physical performance standpoint, [Dorothy] brought out the best in all of us. As a teenager I'm like, yeah I guess I'm bringing the best I can forward, but there are a lot of things that go on in your head. There is a lot that comes through that, expression through dance. If you're having trouble in your family, like my parents going through a divorce and my younger siblings were out doing things that weren't healthy for them.

But I had my dance. I relied on it and she was supportive of that, even into young motherhood. She just helped me find my way, so I guess that would be a way to bring the best out of yourself and move forward. She was a confidant, we could talk to Dorothy about things we couldn't talk to other people about and she would provide that platform. One of the most memorable things for me was our times when she would say "Hey we're not going to do class today, we're just going to sit and talk." We would have those times and they weren't that often but they were super meaningful. There were days where we'd be chatting about something and I think she got a sense that it was more important to talk than it was to take class. Then we would do a quick warm-up and go into rehearsal. But there were those times, rare, but super meaningful because you knew that you could talk to her about anything. She was a good listener and she would provide her own personal stories to help us relate to what we might have been going through at that time. It felt like home, and what I mean by that, it was a place where you went, you were accepted. Dorothy's husband Jim was in the kitchen cooking dinner or he might be watching television. I think having a studio in your home helps relay that aura. It felt like home because it was in a family home, but also we were there as sisters and brothers to work hard together and that makes you feel like family.

Her image of this beautiful wise woman, her hair was always a big thing for some reason because her and Kimberli always had these beautiful long locks. Her Native culture, it's amazing to me how deeply I, and I don't know if it's because she kind of transferred that philosophy, but the Native culture has become such a very strong part of my own life. We have a lot of Native baskets and artwork— and I do think that her presence, that representation even though she didn't talk about being Native, there were very few times that she talked about that, but it's that pride. She's very proud, the way she holds herself up, it's a deep thing. It's so ingrained that you absorb it whether you talk about it or not. It's something that you can stand twenty feet away from her and feel, it's just remarkable.

She used to swear at us on stage and be smoking her cigarette. In the early days of teaching, she would smoke cigarettes while teaching, and while we were up on stage rehearsing she'd yell out "You look like shit!"

MELISSA ESAU *was Dorothy's student from the 60s to the early 80s.*

I started with Dorothy when I was eight and I danced for ten years with her. I left to go to school, got married, and then I came back about seven years later. I danced for three more years until I got pregnant with my first child and then I left. I actually started with another dance studio that Dorothy had danced with, they were all sort of together.

The dance teacher said, "If Melissa really wants to pursue this then she needs to go dance with Dorothy because Dorothy is going to be professional and get her ready for that kind of career." When I started with Dorothy I basically had to start all over again with my training and work my way up. I started with two ballet lessons a week and as I got older I would add another. I auditioned for the company when I was twelve or thirteen and got into the company, which at that time was San Joaquin Concert Ballet Company. We were all in it together, Elizabeth, Beth Keller, Beth Main, Marcia, we were all together, we were that group of dancers. We spent five, six, seven years dancing in the company with Dorothy. I think you'll see this as you talk to everybody, Dorothy was tough so you either got on the bandwagon or you got out: it was baptism by fire. If you couldn't handle it, you probably weren't going to be there very long and not because of her, but because you made that decision not to dance with her anymore.

Back in those days, the 60s and 70s, the arts community was super vibrant in [Stockton], you had the ballet company which was Dorothy's, you had the Stockton Opera Association, you had the Stockton Symphony, and you had Stockton Civic Theater. You had other things but those were the four big organizations— they all had a board of directors and a lot of people supported all four of them. It was big, Dorothy had a board of directors and had worked to develop this company because she always wanted a professional ballet company in this town. That was her goal, that's still her goal at 90 years old, that's what she always wanted and God bless her for that, I mean she's 90, she doesn't even look 90. She wanted to have that and that's how she trained us. When you signed that contract you were there five days a week and then you had rehearsals on Saturday and Sunday for whatever ballets you were working on. I did that from the time I was 13 to the time I was 18— I went to school and I went to dance, that was my life. And that was your life if you made that decision, because if you didn't want that then you couldn't make the commitment.

This is not a bad thing or a good thing but it shows you how meticulous she was about ballets. One thing that I learned and I think everyone will tell you is that we learned discipline; the discipline that she taught us was about making yourself do something to the best of your ability. We never had competition within each other even though we probably did, but it wasn't really obvious. She didn't ever put us one against the other, because the competition was always within ourselves. So if you were doing an exercise and she said you needed to get your leg up to a 90 degree, next time you do it see if you can get it up to 95 degrees. So you were always trying to make yourself better and competing with yourself to be better, to be the best, to make yourself do it correctly.

TERRY PAGO *was Dorothy's student from the early 70s to the early 80s.*
I started in 1971. We had a different kind of relationship because I danced for her but I also choreographed for her. The last time I danced for her was in the late 70s but I did do a piece for her in the early 80s— I've been in and out of her life for the past 20 or 30 years. When I first started my intention was to become an actor and do some theater, and I didn't have the best structure. So nobody would work with me, nobody would cast me in any shows, if I did get cast in any shows it was a two-liner or a one-liner. I never got any major roles, so thought *Fuck it, I'll just dance.*
So I get in touch with Dorothy Percival, and I am this child that just has no center whatsoever. Dorothy has a good sense of people and she basically took me under her wing and developed me. Not particularly as a dancer because I didn't have the actual talent, my dance ability was maybe a step below mediocre. But she used me well, and there is always this point with Dorothy Percival where she has to have the talk with you the same way she has with the girls. The talks she would have with the girls is "I don't think you'll get hired as a professional dancer, is there anything else that you are interested in, in the dance field that I

can assist you with?" So I was not very talented, I was just a guy who got to dance a few roles.

CHAPTER 9

A Complex Relationship

Throughout the sixties, Dorothy was being pulled between three studios and practically living and breathing ballet. But this inevitably began to put a strain on her home life. Since Dorothy was always "Dorothy Percival the Ballet Instructor," it seems she may have had a hard time being Dorothy Percival the Wife and Mother when she got home.

BETH MAIN
I had wondered this as an adult, I never wondered it at the time, because Kimberli and Tamara were always in class with us. And I never saw Dorothy give them… She didn't treat them differently, I was never aware that they were Dorothy's daughters. Everyone was treated the same, but it didn't occur to me until recent years that all that Dorothy poured into all of this, into all of us, her many, countless daughters and sons must surely have taken away from her actual daughters.

KIMBERLI CAMPBELL

[Dorothy] has a very strong personality, which I think given the things that she has done, has to be an asset for a person. She never ever let anything stop her— and I think my dad was almost a perfect union even though I think they didn't get along a lot of times like a lot of parents do. It was a perfect union because he sort of let her— not that he let her because she didn't have anybody let her do anything. But he was accepting of her intensity. I'm sure they had their own altercations behind the scenes that as kids we weren't aware of. I mean they had unhappy periods, she had left him for a year. It wasn't my dad leaving my mom, it was my mom leaving my dad. I don't know if it had anything to do with work, marriages are personal. I just know that one day my mom came and checked me out of school in the fifth grade and we moved. We moved into an apartment and it was a matter of months, maybe eight or nine months, something like that. Maybe almost a year, so the fifth grade and when I was in the sixth grade they were back together. But yeah there was a separation and it's hard for kids, but to understand it and to know why sure led to a different perspective.

But they went back together and things kept going— we used to wonder why they were married, then in the end when you look back, the relationship worked. I don't know how they made it work, he was willing to be what she needed him to be. He helped her a lot at the recitals for a long time, he was working behind the scenes and running the lights, and doing the stage managing, he did a lot of that supporting her.

Sometimes when you look back things are a lot rosier than when you're living in them but then also from a kid's perspective you view different things you know? There was a lot of volatility sometimes but they made it work and made it through 50 plus years so something clicked.

TAMARA WAGNER

It became a problem later when I was a teenager because I didn't have a real good attitude towards her in class and so she clamped down on that real hard, in front of people of course. I wouldn't say that the expectations of me were any higher really than anybody else. I always worked really hard for the most part, not as hard as I could be all the time. But I was encouraged to work harder if I wasn't doing it because she understood what my potential was, and what I was capable of. We had our own personal problems but I wouldn't say that she actually treated me differently. I think that she lost her temper at me a couple of times because I wasn't being respectful.

Not much was happening personally, there wasn't much communication. She was in the house, but of a temperament that didn't really make her approachable.

I think that [ballet] brought us [Kimberli and Tamara] closer together because we both had very different strengths and weaknesses so... It was something we got to do together and we spent a lot of time together. And I think that that was good and it definitely had a lot to do with my relationship with my sister now and our relationship to our mother.

I was so young when I started training with her, like five years old, so I was just used to the whole routine of going to class and being the student and all of that stuff. We took some fun trips together, her and I and my sister places that she wanted to go visit. And we all got along, her and I and my sister when we were all doing that.

I asked Tamara if she would have done ballet even if her mom hadn't had done it.

I don't know if I would have been exposed to it [ballet]. But probably so because I have some natural abilities that I could use in that area- but it takes a long time for you to understand that when you're young and going through being a teenager. I always liked to dance, I didn't always like the hard work, I liked the music, I liked doing all the performing and all of that.

I asked Tamara about a fond memory that she had of working with her mother where everything just sort of clicked.

It would be any memory that I had of being in a piece in which I was successful and able to do pretty well and so was in her favor. Wasn't getting in trouble, I was always able to do what needed to be done just kind of naturally. So any memory that was positive like that was good, that was one of the only ways I got attention and positive feedback. I mean don't get me wrong my mother always loved me, It's just that she was always into her own thing and so sometimes we weren't getting what we needed as children growing up and stuff. It became an issue as time went on.

I think I was trained pretty early to detect and take care of my own issues if I felt insecure or bad about the way I was treated in class or something. I was never allowed to express that, so the message from a pretty early time was *I'm not really interested in how this is affecting you emotionally.* Because what was important was the finished product, it was me as a dancer and my performance and respecting her in front of people.

I asked if she ever brought this up in later years.

She thinks I just don't like her because she made me work hard. It's hard to go to a place like that with her because she gets pretty defensive and she's never wrong. It will always turn into some kind of confrontation and I learned pretty young to fear confrontation because that is just what I got and I didn't like it. It made me uncomfortable, it made me unhappy and so I didn't say much to her. It would be like complaining about something that she is not going to change and can't do anything about or won't do anything about.

I asked Tamara about her father.

Yeah, my father was easier on me, he wasn't my instructor for one thing, and he was just a little more accessible. But then if I tried to complain about my mother, which I never did, we got that message very young. He didn't want to hear about it, not really, until later in my 30's or whatever, where he admitted that she was very particular and perfectionist about when I was being raised as a child. The expectations were high, you know she was a disciplinarian with very specific ideas about how children should be raised and how they should behave, very authoritarian. And that really couldn't be argued.

You know, I think that she is a very talented person, but I think she has some other issues that make it difficult for her to get along or take advice from anyone, not just me. As a parent you had your child there, they couldn't say "Oh Dorothy I think you're being too hard on our kids" or "I don't like what you said to our daughter." People didn't do that, they just pulled them out because she would be confrontational. She doesn't take criticism, or she would take everything as criticism.

I asked if these feelings drove her more in ballet.

Some of those feelings? I don't know, I got to be a pretty angry young woman and so I just danced real hard because I was really mad. I mean if I had wanted to, my sister had stopped dancing when she was around 19 and if I had wanted to I think if I said "I really don't want to do this." Or if I had zero talent then and all that sort of thing then she would have said "Fine." But that wasn't the case, I was the one who got pushed.

CHAPTER 10

Pushing Her Students

E LIZABETH ARCHER
We had a lot of good, hard times together, but we were all close. It was interesting because we really didn't go to school together, but coming from different places in Stockton and or Lodi. But we got in the studio and through that learning to accept each others differences, different body shapes, different abilities, different ways of thinking, different looks. And because you're all working together towards a common goal and a common passion, you do become very close. And you share a lot of things, physically or mentally.

MARCIA HENDRICKS *danced with Dorothy from 1971 through 1977.*
I danced with Dorothy '71 through '75 and a little bit of '77. I have to share that I was really late to starting ballet. I had to beg my mother for lessons for many years but she wanted me to play the piano. So I actually started doing ballet with Margret Smallie who was well known in the community area that I lived in. I went to school with her son and my best friend took ballet

from her. But I had always been an athletic kid and always well
put together, and strong, and motivated, and loved to move.
When I sat at the piano I really wanted to move to that music
so I accelerated in my training with Mrs. Smallie and that fall of
'70 she suggested that I audition for San Joaquin Concert Ballet.
Which I thought was kind of silly because I had only two years
of ballet and I was just starting pointe work. But we looked at it
like it would just be an experience with no expectations, but I
actually got accepted as an apprentice. And that year was kind
of a whirlwind because there were sicknesses and illnesses that
propelled me to be casted in ballets that were kind of over my
head quite honestly. But I guess Dorothy saw my tenaciousness
and that I was going to work hard— and yes one of the ballets
had to be a little bit choreographed so I started in one group at
the first part and ended in another. It's funny because the ballet
was titled *Portraits* so it starts with a portrait of these classical people in a certain position but in the end I had to be in a
different position because I had to be woven in and out for what
I could do, and for someone else had to pick up and do to cover
the person who was ill or injured. So I guess I started working
with her by the seat of my pants, you know? I really respected
her, she was demanding, she really expected musicality and the
court of ballet [ballet de cour] to be perfectly in sync. Which
to this day it still bugs me when I see a company and I see that
people aren't in sync. That bothers me, but anyway.
I kind of recognized the value that I might need to up my training, so over the next couple of years I actually started to take
from both teachers. As a member of the company, you automat-
ically got company class and you had rehearsals on Saturdays so

there was a lot of movement augmenting your Monday through Friday training.

I made good friends and I just felt like it was a really good group of people to be a part of. And so I was really excited the following year when I auditioned I actually got in as a member, not an apprentice so I felt like that was goal achieved. But through all that I always felt like I was one step behind, and it was hard at times. I really learned that ballet is not fair because I didn't often get parts that I had hoped to or had gotten a part and then I got switched out- you know there were other situations that were out of our control.

There was an instance where we did a very provocative piece that we had auditioned for, I don't know if you're familiar with the regional ballet movement that we were a part of. We were an up-and-coming youth ballet company that was starting to get honor status. But there was a large piece that we did that was deep and a little racy for parts and so the adjudicators wanted it to be pared way down, and so I lost my part in that as many people did.

It was hard because I always felt like I was chasing after that carrot and maybe wasn't the most flexible, I certainly wasn't the long tall, skinny type of the era. So there were pressures to be thin, there were periods of time where we had weigh ins and as my body developed, it's just my genetic pattern. I'm large busted and I often got cues to make sure I had good bras so that I wouldn't bounce on stage. I'm grateful that I had enough love and support around because I probably had what you would call disordered eating, but I'm grateful that I did not go down the path of an eating disorder. I did not go bulimic, I did not go anorexic but there was always this pressure to be thin by performance time and I know that was hard and I think it was hard on everybody. But there was that threshold that was expected. I am absolutely not a wallflower. I'm very put-myself-out-there, don't-give-up-work-hard. I guess I would say I wasn't amongst the chosen ones. When I talk about those women that got all the great parts, because they had the great bodies and they had trained for years ahead of me. They just had the advantage plus they have the genetics.

One of my daughter's dance teachers here in Walnut Creek was like, "Sorry, but dancers are born." And you know you can't remake your body completely. So I guess I just definitely felt like I wasn't in the top tier - I was a strong core dancer, I was not a soloist. At times, there were some little pieces where I got little solos, but I just wasn't elevated to that status. But it was okay, I just strive to do my best and have fun. And I gained a lot by being in that group.

And I think everybody might say that- when you train for something that seriously, you learn a lot of discipline and you learn that you have to move on if it doesn't go your way. You try to stay healthy and not get injured. And they've gotten a lot better about that these days, you know?

(What was the hardest time that Dorothy ever pushed you?)
I would say it was about the weight. You need to lose weight or not gain weight, or you're not going to be a member. Yeah, it was definitely over body type. It's really hard because I'm five-three. I probably have been five-three, ever since I was in seventh grade. People would say that I look fit right now. And I'm 130. But for dancing I was expected to be under 115.

It was hard for my body. Because I felt like I met all my other benchmarks. You know, I had good attendance. I worked hard in class. I didn't give attitude. When I first started with Dorothy it was the era where she had the stick that she would pound out the meter to things but she also might point with her stick at your body where you needed to straighten. Quite honestly in the early days she still smoked in the studio too.

I wanted to share the fun and fond memories about jazz classes on Friday nights because I think we just got to let our hair down and just be our personalities. I think Dorothy loved doing it just as much with us. We'd often be doing contemporary music of the time. She really liked to put a groove on for the time. And when I made reference to that piece that was considered a little racy, it was considered our jazz piece.

The hard thing about jazz being on Friday nights was that it kept us out of our social life you know? I can remember not wanting to miss jazz on Friday night and then switching into clothes to get to a football game, to try and have a high school life. The jazz classes were kind of a hoot. Some of the top shelf ballerinas, they just could not find their hips and have a groove so I guess that was a little bit of a leveling field sometimes. Because there were some of us that were just a little better at jazz, or felt sexy, I don't know. Jazz classes were fun and kind of an equalizer of the field a little bit.

CHERYLL KERR *was Dorothy's student from late 70s to the mid 80s.*

I met Dorothy when I was about nine years old. I still studied at a studio in Stockton called Ms. Lavernes. She only taught up to a certain level and Dorothy was teaching more professional-level classes so I ended up switching over to her school.

[*The Nutcracker*] was great. It was very exciting as a kid— it was probably the biggest moneymaker you could do in Stockton because it's such a small town. So it was a big thing every year and I started out as a bear in the toy scene and a child in the party scene. And then when I was around 11, or 12 and 13 they started doing the other roles. I did Arabian the last year I was there, snowflake, and flowers.

It was exciting, Dorothy really put on a very professional production with great costumes. The costume closet was always an exciting super fun thing to do where she had all the costumes for all her productions and it was really magical, it was great.

Dorothy really promoted creativity and spontaneity. I remember when she would hold auditions, she would say, 'Okay well who wants to audition for Clara?' and nobody would hold up their hand because we were all too shy.

She taught me about discipline, how to discipline myself and how to be disciplined, and how to work hard. She was really amazing at that and would ask, "What do you want to be next year?" or "What do you want to be this year?" She would always encourage you to reach for the stars, and go after what you want.

I was nine years old when I started, so I idolized her. She was very matter-of-fact, she was very detail-oriented, and she was a hard teacher. She expected you to work hard, if you were going to be in her class you had to pay attention. There was no slacking off. You had to work hard and she really responded to that and encouraged you to be the best you could be.

Once, I found myself in an advanced class at a young age, around 12 or 13. There was a moment when I struggled with a combination or something similar, and Dorothy made it clear that if I wasn't willing to work hard, I shouldn't return to that particular class. It really struck a chord with me, and I couldn't hold back my tears.

Looking back, though, I realize that experience served as a catalyst for me to push myself even harder. She always gave me special attention since I was a scholarship student, although not a full one. Taking classes every day was a financial challenge for my parents, but she generously invested her time and attention in me, making it possible for me to continue my education. But even though I was a scholarship student, she expected that same kind of hard work from everyone.

I idolized Dorothy. I wanted to be a part of her ballet company, her apprentice company, and her main ballet company. She expected you to work your hardest and if you did that, then that was good with her. She made me who I am today.

She instilled self-confidence in me and taught me the values of discipline, hard work, and a strong work ethic. When I was 13, my parents decided that I should prioritize my studies, and it broke my heart to leave. However, I later reconnected with Dorothy, and the lessons she imparted to me have shaped my entire life. I wouldn't have achieved what I have or become the person I am today without her guidance and teachings. The wisdom I gained at such a young age extends far beyond the ballet studio and has been invaluable. Dorothy gave me gifts that even my own parents couldn't provide.

She just had a very strong personality and she believed if you're going to do something, do it well. And she taught that and expected that of us. It taught me if I was gonna do anything, do it well, or don't do it at all. If you're not going to try hard, don't waste your own time. It's a wonderful life lesson.

Me, personally, I'm so grateful to her for everything that she taught me. I only spent five or six years studying with her when I was that age. And I did come back and take a few classes with her at Delta College and things like that later. But those formative years when she gave me guidance and attention: they're the base of the self-esteem that I was able to develop as a woman later. I don't think I would be the same person if I had not met Dorothy, and I'm so grateful to her for that.

There's a big difference between teaching children, young adults, and teenagers for a professional career and teaching 20-year-olds. Adult ballet is a very different environment so she was probably more laid back in the Delta classes. And I didn't do them for very long because I ended up moving to Sacramento, and dancing there and eventually in San Francisco, New York, and London.

I pursued dancing until my early 30s, even performing semi-professionally in Sacramento and San Francisco. However, in my mid-20s, I made the decision to embark on a different career path.

Nonetheless, I never stopped dancing. No matter where I traveled, I carried with me the invaluable lessons taught by my mentor. Her unwavering pursuit of perfection and her meticulous teaching style instilled in me a strong foundation and impeccable technique. People worldwide would compliment me on my beautiful and precise execution, acknowledging the impact of her teaching.

Dorothy never settled for mediocrity; she molded dancers to be disciplined and refined. If you were attentive and receptive, her instruction proved to be immensely rewarding. She was a true master of her craft and had a profound influence on shaping my life.

Dorothy taught me how to be a perfectionist, I couldn't do what I do today without that. I'm well-known in my field as a freelance court reporter, I take depositions in very high-level commercial litigation cases. So intellectual property, patent, and copyright litigation as well as multimillion-dollar banking cases. These cases that you see in the news these days such as cryptocurrency cases require attention to detail.

Just like in Dorothy's class, you can't slack off—if you're going to do it, do it and do it well. I've built my career on that and I feel like Dorothy gave me everything I have, because I couldn't have done any of it without her teaching me to be so disciplined and work so hard.

ELIZABETH ARCHER
(I asked if Dorothy was good at rallying the troops.)
Yeah, because she was our center, she was kind of the heart of it all, you have to have a big heart.
(What was Dorothy's personality like?)
Strict and hard, [Dorothy] used to have a cane, we all talk about the cane. But it was just so amazing to be able to learn how my body worked. From everything: from your little finger to your little toe, you knew how to control your body- and it was

through that refinement, and through that work, and through her eyes as a technician. What it means to reach, what it means to dance with full passion through a technical perspective. She just inspired, she could see things in people, she knew dancers' capabilities, and she drove those dancers through that potential. So she could see what each of us were good at, and she brought that to the table.

MELISSA ESAU

For as tough as Dorothy was, especially when you grew up with her, and literally all of us, grew up with her. If we weren't at home with our parents, we were with Dorothy. So Dorothy really took us through our formidable years, you know, preteen teenager, all that stuff. She was there with us. So she had an insight to each one of us. She knew how to get us to do what we needed to do. She knew how hard to be on us. When to back off, and she would sense sometimes if you were not having a good day, she would say things like, "Did you have a bad day at school today?" And maybe you didn't, and maybe you did, and you didn't realize it? But evidently she sensed it. You would say "No, it was good." or "Yeah, I had a bad day." So she knew how far to push you on what days and when to kick your butt on the other days. And there were days, she had to kick your butt. But like I said, if you didn't like it, you could always leave, and that's just how it was.

In my opinion, what a lot of people could learn from this is that you could never be late, not even a minute. If you were not in the inner studio, ready to go by the time she was ready to go, don't come up the stairs late because there was a waiting room downstairs. And you better be going up the stairs with everybody else. Because if you were late, don't come up the stairs, and you learned punctuality, not only punctuality, but you learned to be early, to be warmed up, and to be ready to go when she was ready to go. Because if you didn't, you'd hear about it and that stuck with me.

I would rather be an hour early than one minute late to anything and I raised my kids that way. It's just rude, it's not considerate of other people, and I think a lot of people could benefit from that today. That was not something that she said, you picked up on that real quick. It just, it was an on-set rule that you were ready to go in on time. And, you know that's what you want your employees to be like, or anybody: be on time, be ready to go and do your job.

TERRY PAGO

We were around her [Dorothy] so much. If she saw something special, if she saw something where we could shine, she promoted everybody to shine. I was probably one of her most promoted people. I'm sure she fought to get her way, I'm sure I got a few scholarships from her recommendations.

But how she most supported me was the times that I would be making dances; she was the perfect person to work with for me. The small success that I did have is basically due to her tweaking things and fixing things and for me to rethink them. So that was basically the support that I got from her.

In that venue, she let me do anything I wanted and she didn't say she didn't "poopoo" it. I came up with a couple of bad ballets that she made. She worked on two, so they actually looked decent, but by all means they weren't any good. I've forgotten all about one of them.

Thank you for reminding me of a bad memory. Don't worry I'm teasing.

CHERYLL KERR

I remember I was in New York in the 1990s. I was living on the Upper East Side and I invited Dorothy to come to see me and she was bringing students to Joffrey Ballet in the summer. She wasn't able to see me that summer but eventually, she came and stayed with me. While I was living in New York, I started flying her when she was getting older to come and bring her students and I would set up an apartment for a week for her. She even spent Christmas one year with me.

I have to say that I think Dorothy is widely misunderstood and has been for years. Every time I talk to Dorothy, she does nothing but remind me how much she loves me and how much she misses me and wants to come see me or wants me to come see her. If I had any problem, and I showed up at her door, no questions asked, she would say 'Come on in, how long can you stay?' She's such a motherly person. And she's a very opinionated person, but she's a survivor. She has been through so many things in life. I mean she's in her 90's now. She expects a lot, she expects respect and she deserves respect.

She and I are similar in a lot of ways. I don't like to cook with other people in my kitchen. If I'm going to be in the kitchen, cooking the meal, I'm in charge. I don't want anyone else telling me how to do it because I know how to do it and Dorothy is very similar. When she is running the show don't tell her what to do. She's been doing her thing for a very long time and she knows how to do it very well. She takes pride in that and she deserves respect for that. People have egos, they really do. And Dorothy is not a person who likes to stroke people's egos but what she does do is teach and guide. And that is a gift that every child should have.

I was nine to 13 years old so I wasn't really involved in the administration of the ballet company or anything like that. In every ballet company and every ballet school, there are politics and there are struggles to raise money. Ballet is vastly underfunded and it's easy to criticize someone else when you don't know how to stand in their shoes and run things and do what they do.

Dorothy is a wonderful person and some people don't understand her or take the time to see things from her side. I'd have had no reason to keep in touch with Dorothy all these years after I stopped dancing, if she wasn't so wonderful, and hadn't given me such a huge gift. So I have no reason to criticize Dorothy at all.

Dorothy over the years told me that she fought against prejudice as a woman. All the things that we as women struggle against, and she ran a ballet company very successfully for many years and a school. That's hard and she raised kids and all that stuff at the same time. I'm talking about all the struggles of life, I'm not talking about any kind of personal struggles.

Life is not easy, especially for a woman, you guys have no idea. It's hard, anything that you want to do that you don't have a man by your side you have to work twice as hard to get what you want as a woman. And then God forbid people see you doing it by yourself.

There's always a struggle to get any kind of recognition for hard work as a woman. It's not easy and people are always trying to take you down. And Dorothy has helped so many kids over the years, given free classes to kids who couldn't afford them, given guidance and encouragement to kids that their parents would just drop them off. They come to Dorothy and they turn out productive, interesting, and successful people—she's amazing.

ELIZABETH ARCHER

(I asked if she danced with Tamara and Kimberli)

I was younger, I was with the company when they were there and taking classes of course, for probably two to three years before they left to do other things. Tamara was always teaching, she went on to teach - Kimberli and I to this day are very close friends.

She's one of my dearest friends and we still stay in touch and don't get to see each other as much as we'd nearly like to that's for sure. We don't live that far but you know, life. But we do communicate through text messages and phone calls still. We're very good friends and our kids used to play together. I had two boys and she has five girls, her younger girls were the same age as my boys. So we did a lot together in those young mother years, had lunches together and supported each other so she's a very special friend.

KIMBERLI CAMPBELL

[Dorothy] was very strict. She was very strict and I think maybe in a way a little harder on myself and my sister than on other students because of the relationship. If you have a parent as a coach they can really drill down on you and get away with it. She was very demanding, was very critical - which dance has to have. Perfection is a hard thing to come by and you always have to strive for it. To be striving for perfection under your dance teacher's eyes is one thing but combine that with your mother's eyes: I think that's a very complex relationship.

My sister and I, we started teaching for her when we were still living at home. I was probably fourteen, maybe? And so was my sister. We taught on Saturdays mostly because there was no school and it seems to me that my mom was involved with the Sacramento Ballet Company at the time so she would go to do dance and rehearsal in Sacramento. And when we were younger, we would go with her and spend our days hanging out in the waiting room while she did class or rehearsal. And when we got older, we started teaching on the weekends and stay home, so I taught for a long time for her in that studio.

I taught tap and ballet, and she had another studio at the Commodore theater, the old Stockton Junior High auditorium that I taught at. At one point she wanted to establish another dance school in Linden so she rented a space and taught there. Then again in Galt, she started a school for me here, you know she fronted the money but I did not do that for very long.

It wasn't very good and it wasn't prosperous, I wasn't as aggressive with the marketing and I don't think my passion was there. So yeah a lot of years of teaching. I could teach now probably and she's right, I think about that if it came right down to it and I needed to do something for somebody I could probably teach dance. I could teach tap or ballet. Oh, and gymnastics, I did that too.

TAMARA WAGNER

I started instructing in the summers when I was around, probably 20 or 21. I started running her summer programs while [Dorothy] would be traveling, I believe I got paid for it. So I did that for a few years for her during the summer. And then eventually I ended up helping out more. By this time, I'm like, older, other goals and you know, not dancing that much and stuff. So my sister and I started teaching some ballet and some tap when we were about 16.

I was born in 1950. And that was when I was 16. So that would be 1966. It was in the 60s.

KIMBERLI CAMPBELL

I remember starting when I was very, very small. I remember. Because after I talked to you, the first few days ago, whatever, I thought: oh, when was the first time I remember even going to a dance studio?

And I remember being maybe four or five, I have this memory in my head of getting out of a car and going into this little dance studio. And the teacher's name was Mrs. Roberts, and she ran a little preschool Dance Studio in Stockton. It was across from what used to be the old state hospital. And I remember getting out of this car, I feel like I was crying, but I don't really know. So that's my first memory of being taken into a little dance studio where this older lady taught dance. And maybe my mom was teaching there too at the time, you know, because I was maybe, I don't know, maybe four or something, very small. And my sister obviously was a couple of years older than me.

So that was my first memory, then I kind of went through a lot of phases with ballet. I never really was like, totally passionate about it. I was always kind of messing up and screwing around and getting in trouble, but that wasn't an option not to do it, not to dance. I always wanted to ride horses or have a horse, or go skiing or do different things like that. Those were not options because they didn't sort of fit into that lifestyle I guess. I never had aspirations of professionalism in any way shape or form But my sister was kind of brought along into a lot of more intense practice. Dance did give us the opportunities: I went to Europe, to Holland with my mom and followed a dance teacher that was teaching there, and went up to Canada to a dance school up there, and went to New York because she was doing that so we got a lot of opportunities out of it.

But specifically for me, to be aspirational about dance itself that was never my personal goal but I'm sure my mom has told you that from the time she can remember I said I wanted to grow up, get married and have 12 kids. She likes to tell that story and I think that maybe that was my counter to my existence at that time without realizing it. I don't want to do this, I want to do that, generational flips.

I remember doing all that and having all those opportunities, which when I look back on it's amazing. [Dorothy] looks back on her life and sees all the things that she was able to go and do and experience and I stopped and think about it for myself. Because of her, all of those things that I did get to do, even though

I didn't get to do this or I didn't get to that. But look what opportunities or experiences I had instead.

CHAPTER 11

Dorothy Goes to College

Dorothy described her daily routine in the early 1970s as going from teaching at her studio and then immediately getting ready to go dance with the Sacramento ballet, only surviving on a pack of peanut M&M's (her favorite). It was clear her schedule was hectic.

Dorothy's already packed schedule was about to get even more hectic. She had received a call from a gentleman by the name of Dr. Laurie, the head of the physical education department at San Joaquin Delta College. A junior college located in Stockton, California.

"Dorothy Percival?" asked Dr. Laurie.

"Yes sir?" replied Dorothy.

Dorothy had already had her regional ballet company and her honor company which was basically consuming her life. But as Dorothy puts it, "It's just growth."

Dr. Laurie told Dorothy his reason for calling: "I'm thinking about putting a dance department at Delta College for ballet."

"Oh good, I was wondering why you didn't have one yet," said Dorothy, since all the other colleges and universities in the state had already had a ballet program. Dorothy explained that one of the reasons ballet became so popular on college campuses was due to the benefits it provided athletes when it comes to practicing balance and technique.

"Would you be interested in talking to me about it?" asked Dr. Laurie.

The elated Dorothy responded with "Sure, I'll talk to anybody about dance, especially ballet."

They made the appointment and Dorothy met with him at his office. Dr. Laurie picked Dorothy's brain about what would be required to open a ballet school at Delta. As their conversation ended Dorothy got up to leave, and just as she was opening the door Dr. Laurie asked, "Would you be interested in doing it?"

Dorothy turned around. "Sure, I would be interested in anything that says ballet or dance."

Dorothy was once again about to leave when he asked "Wait, Dorothy, what's your degree?"

She then thought that was the end of it. "Oh, I guess that takes care of it."

"Why?" asked Dr. Laurie.

"I have no degree." answered Dorothy.

"You have no degree?"

"No sir, I was too busy learning, and none of the schools or universities had what I needed."

Dr. Laurie was surprised, because Dorothy had many accomplishments up to this point with ballet companies. "Are you sure you have no degree?"

"No I have no degree, I didn't go to college. There was nothing there that could serve me to do what I needed for me."

"Oh…"

"I guess that takes care of that problem."

"No, I think I can take care of that."

Dr. Laurie's solution was to give Dorothy an eminence credential that lasted for over twenty years, and when she retired so did the credential.

At this point Dorothy was ready.

"When do we start?" she asked.

"Come back in the middle of August." replied Dr. Laurie

Once again Dorothy moved to leave, but Dr. Laurie called her back in and asked, "Wait Dorothy, don't you want to know how much money you're going to make?"

Surprised, Dorothy asked, "You're going to pay me?"

Dr. Laurie sat back down in his chair and began to laugh. "Of course," he said.

"Well nobody has ever said they were going to pay me."

In the arts, you often work for free, so Dorothy was never paid for being the artistic director for various shows or any of the other projects she worked on. The only thing she ever got paid for was her lessons so this came as a shock to Dorothy.

Later that August the construction began on the studio room at Delta College, which Dorothy (of course) oversaw to make sure it was done correctly. During this process, her strive for perfection came out. When the construction crew began laying the floor for her studio, it wasn't up to par, so she had them tear the floor up and lay it down again in order for it to have the proper "bounce."

After Dorothy began teaching at Delta College, she also received an offer to teach at the University of the Pacific (UOP), a private university in Stockton, California which also happens to be the first chartered university in the state's history.

"I was asked to go teach at UOP. I said yes, I only had one day that was free. I said yes and enrolled a few of the girls and so forth. I'm just not a babysitter for rich kids. That's what it was like, little rich girls would come and maybe be dressed and maybe not. I'm sorry, I told [UOP's dean]. I don't even remember what his name was. I said I've never quit a job in my life, but I am not a babysitter for rich kids. You don't pay me enough." explained Dorothy.

Dorothy left UOP after a short time and focused on her own company and her position at Delta College. Her story with UOP was not done there however, as she hosted many of her ballets in UOP's main auditorium, some of them I attended in the later years including *The Nutcracker* and *Lon Po Po*, a Chinese version of *Little Red Riding Hood*. As we wrapped up this portion of the interview Dorothy said "Rich doesn't mean you have talent." And seeing where Dorothy came from, nobody would know that more than her.

MARCIA HENDRICKS

There were definitely people that felt like it wasn't worth putting up with, there were those who were like, "No, I'm not getting anything out of this."

And I don't know if some of it was that I had those other days of the week at Margret Smallie's studios, and she definitely was a completely different personality. I don't know if that was kind of a good balance that maybe I didn't have it all there.

Because I think that there were some girls that experienced a
lot of stress from the expectations that Dorothy had for them.
But I also learned later, there were good reasons that some
girls were there because they were having some hard things in
their family. And I think that she had emphasized empathy and
cared for us.

I had a situation when I was at UC Santa Barbara that I lost a
good friend, she was a victim of being kidnapped and murdered, there were actually three girls that were kidnapped and
murdered in Santa Barbara, it was a very scary time. I just
was really stressed out and was getting ulcers. It wasn't like I
feared going outside my door but I was just not coping with the
academic stress and these personal stresses that were going on.
So I took a leave of absence from UC Santa Barbara and I came
home for a semester and went to Delta College. And Dorothy
immediately invited me back into the company. And she gave
me a job to do, actually two jobs, that basically were the trade
off to pay my tuition. So I thought that was a real act of grace.
It seems to me, we always had one class at Delta during the
week. In my own healing, I think I needed structure, I needed
to be back in a fold of people. I mean, I was also grateful for
very dear friends that I had gone to high school with, who were
in their second year at Delta college, with plans to transfer. But I
had one of them went and registered for me, so that when I got
there, late January, I had classes.

And another friend showed up the first day of school to show
me all around campus. So I just felt like, between my family, my
friends, and my ballet family, it really got me back on my feet.
And so I was able to go back my junior year at UC Santa Bar-

bara without having lost ground. So I was able to graduate on time, and I kept my grade point average up, because getting into physical therapy schools is super competitive, so you have to have great grades and blah, blah, blah.

That was definitely something that I felt was an act of grace for her to just invite me back in, and I had been taking classes in Santa Barbara.

I tried to double major, I auditioned to be in the dance department thinking that I could do that and the prerequisites I would need for PT school. And they— at the end of the audition, I was not one of the ones that they selected and I felt really let down because you know. My opinion was in the room I had some pretty decent technique and was better than many or whatever, but they just didn't like the idea that my sole focus wasn't dance. Not classical ballet, but they still have classical ballet in their curriculum. And the teacher who was responsible for teaching ballet, came over to me and personally invited me to take his classes. And I don't remember if he knew Dorothy who was or what, or he just maybe felt for me. But I was able to continue to take ballet all through my freshman and beginning of my sophomore year.

So in being invited back to the company, it wasn't like I had been on hiatus for an entire year, but I hadn't been doing pointe work. So the one caveat is that I rejoined the company for that semester, but I wasn't cast in anything that was pointe work. I do have to say I did have one kind of main solo thing. We had done an outreach program, with schools doing Peter and the Wolf. And Dorothy had envisioned that the wolf would be this boxing character, like with gloves, kind of dog-like, and, burly. So guess who got the wolf part? I shared it with Beth Keller. That was a really fun thing and people really liked what I brought to that role. So I guess I got some funny attention in that way. It made a plus thing to come back and do that.

I think I was in *Duck Soup* on that one too, which was a kind of a silly jazz ballet. If I didn't have my descendent genetics of being short with bigger breasts than what I needed, because I have long legs. I shared as an adult with some other adults that I had danced with, I said ``Well, this was what, you know, held me back." and they were just shocked. And I was like, "Well, it was the times." You know, back then you just needed to be real thin. And I just never could look rail thin.

I never remember getting any counseling on nutrition, it wasn't done. All the dance medicine stuff is so different today. I guess I just figured out that I needed to eat protein and you know, stay away from chips and french fries, all those things that kids want to pig out on by going to McDonald's after a football game, you know, or something like that.

I think this one thing helped me keep my body lean was, you know in the era that I went to Stockton Junior High School, we were expected to take city buses to and from school. They were always jammed, full, pretty disgusting, whatever.

I early on got hooked on cycling to school. So I lived by Anderson Park, and I think one way to Stockton Junior High was about four miles. So I cycled four miles to and from school, eight miles round trip every day through that era. So I think that really helped me to stay lean, as lean as I could. And then it was a matter of just drinking diet sodas rather than having regular sodas or I would have fruit and yogurt with granola. I had a little bit of help in that era too, my own father was diagnosed as a type two diabetic. So my mom had been counseled dietary wise on changing things. And so, probably, that was helpful too that I think my mom was presenting more low carb meals: we just had a little better sense of what good nutrition was.

Even as an adult, as I said, my mom, it's just a genetic thing, we have a predisposition to type two diabetes, so I'm careful. In my life work as a physical therapist, you kind of want to practice what you preach, right? I've never felt like I've had a weight problem as an adult, I mean, people would not describe me as having a weight problem. And again, it's just, I think, from some habits early on, and enjoying being active.

I can't take classical ballet anymore, my hips don't, like, turn out. But a friend of mine was laid off during the summer with the COVID stuff. She has more of a like, Latin fusion-leaning [style] and was teaching classes. And she had made a connection through her flamenco teacher with a flamenco teacher in Madrid, Spain. And so she pushed or peddled this class to a bunch of us, where we actually took online classes where she warmed us up with her kind of Latin salsa, jazz stuff. And then the flamenco teacher took over and we were learning flamenco. And that was great fun while it lasted, and then my friend got rehired and we haven't been able to have our Wednesday morning classes. But you know if there's a form of dance that I can do that doesn't force turnout, I attempt it here and there.

CHAPTER 12

Meeting Norbert Vesak

Dorothy often allowed different choreographers to come to her company in order to choreograph her shows. One of them was the Canadian choreographer Norbert Vesak. Dorothy describes Vesak as a "magnificent choreographer."

Norbert was a massively influential figure in not just Canadian ballet, but ballet around the world. He co-founded the Pacific Dance Theater in Vancouver, BC before going on to found his own studio called the Western Dance Theater (which unfortunately didn't pan out well for him due to financial difficulties). However, this did not stop him from getting work at the Royal Winnipeg Ballet, which happens to be Canada's oldest and most respected ballet company. The company commissioned him for *The Ecstasy of Rita Joe* in 1971 which was funded by the Manitoba Indian Brotherhood, and *What to Do Till the Messiah Comes* in 1973. Vesak and Dorothy crossed paths in 1973 during the Banff Festival of the Arts.

"I met him in Canada at the Banff School of Fine Arts and he did a few ballets there. And he used two of my kids that were on scholarship there that he didn't know were mine— and I had not met him before. So when he found out that they were mine, it made him much more interested in who I was, to begin with. And we became very good friends." explained Dorothy.

Dorothy then asked Vesak about one of the ballets he had choreographed at Banff School of Fine Arts.

"Can I have that ballet for my company here in Stockton?" asked Dorothy.

"Of course," replied Vesak.

In order to put the ballet together at Dorothy's Stockton studio, Vesak would commute from the Bay Area to Dorothy's studio on the weekends. He would repeat this commute every weekend until the show was finished. Dorothy said that every time he would come back and see his ballet being performed, Vesak would look at her and ask "Did I do that, Dorothy?"

"Yes, you sure did," replied Dorothy.

"Boy, I'm good huh?"

"You're really good. You have no idea how good you are, you're really good."

Vesak eventually wrote a ballet called *Butterflies Can't Live Here Anymore*, a pas de deux: meaning a dance for two people, with one of two people being Rico Costa, who was a student for Dorothy during this time. This ballet was chosen for a night gala, which is an arts and entertainment event where high-up public figures attend with the proceeds being donated to charity in some instances. He had given the ballet to a company in Los Angeles and eventually gave it to Dorothy. Vesak got paid anywhere from $16,000 to $20,000 when he let a company use his ballet, but he never charged Dorothy a dime.

"I have five of his ballets for nothing," explained Dorothy.

When Dorothy was offered the ballets for free, she hesitated. But Vesak responded with: "Now wait a minute, you are the only one who does it the way I want."

The Sacramento Ballet wanted to produce Vesak's ballets, and at the time Barbera Crockett was in charge of the company. When Vesak declined their offer, Crockett asked why Vesak would allow Dorothy to produce the ballet but not them. "Well Dorothy has it," said Crockett.

Vesak's retort was: "Yes, but you don't have Dorothy."

Even Dorothy thought this was a little harsh. When he explained the situation to her, she said, "Geez, Norbert."

"Dorothy, you are the only one who directs the way I want."

Dorothy said the reason Vesak preferred working with her over other directors was because she was always very involved in the choreographing phase of Vesak's ballets. She would stand next to him and take notes of the words he used or the expressive ways he would use the words, which would tell Dorothy a lot about what he desired in his ballet.

"I would use HIS words, not mine, to rehearse it and so forth. So what he was seeing was his image… It wasn't my image, it was his image. Because maybe I would see it differently and that would be my ballet, not his. He understood that I understood."

I would love to be able to get Norbert Vesak's perspective on this, but unfortunately he passed on in 1990 at the young age of 53, due to a brain aneurysm. He took with him a valuable perspective on Dorothy's career since he trusted her and nobody else with so much of his work.

At the end of this part of the interview, I could see Dorothy really get sentimental talking about her late friend. She bookended this part of the interview by reminiscing: "A brilliant choreographer, just brilliant, brilliant, brilliant."

Many of Dorothy's students have countless stories of working on Vesak's ballets including Melissa who recalled her time with the ballet *Gift to be Simple*.

MELISSA ESAU

Keeping in mind that it was about the discipline of the art, we were doing a ballet called *Gift to be Simple*, and it was choreographed by Norbert Vesak. I think there were 12 to 14 of us in this ballet and it was based on the Shakers. They were kind of like Quakers but they were the Shakers.

It was probably a 20 to 25-minute ballet, for the opening we were in a "v" with the point upstage, and the opening was three minutes long. We had to make sure that we were in a straight line and when we crossed it was very specific, and the thing about Dorothy is that when you were doing an ensemble you had to be absolutely in line with the person in front of you, you had to be exactly on point with your arms, head, everything. She did not like ensembles to be messy and I agree, I very much like that too.

So the opening was three minutes, we were rehearsing for our May concert and I remember that was the last ballet we were working on that night, we started at like 3:00 or 3:30. We spent, and I'm not kidding you, four hours from 7:00 to 11:00 pm working on this three-minute opening to get it exactly correct with the arms that had to be at the waist, I mean it super specific and everybody's hands had to turn at the same time, the legs had to be the same way. And by the way, we were wearing

25 pounds of costume, the underslip was ten pounds of white cotton that had to twirl it was these big skirts, and then the top part was mattress ticking which was this fabric that they used to cover all mattresses in that was very thick, it was white with blue stripes and it was heavy.

That outer dress was 15 pounds that went from the neck, all the way to the ground, and it was long-sleeved so you had 25 pounds that you had to move and get there on time. So it was very difficult— four hours on three minutes of an opening ballet. That's indicative of how Dorothy was, she would take that amount of time to make sure everything was specific.

Now it's 7:00 at night and you're doing the same thing over, and over, and over again. And you did not want to be that person that got called out because your leg was wrong or your arm was wrong because then we had to do it again because so and so wasn't where they were supposed to be. So by 11:00, you're like 'Can we just get this right?'

But you couldn't say anything: there was no crying, there were no comments, you went back and did it again, and that's just how it was because you didn't need to cry. There was no reason to cry, you couldn't cry. Like I was saying, that's not a good or bad thing, that just shows how much Dorothy wanted every-thing to be perfect in the dancing.

She used to say, and this is an expression that has stayed with me my whole life: "If you only strive for mediocrity, that's all you'll ever get. So you need to always strive for perfection, even though you may not get there, that is what you're working for. Because if you settle for anything less that is all you're go-ing to get."

That is the theme. When we had a reunion, we thought *Oh that's right*. Because we all had stories to tell about our life and growing up and going out into the world, and all those things have stuck with us and made us successful people because of that training that she gave us. Yeah, sometimes it was painful, that's the reality of it, sometimes it was painful and don't mean physically. You had to be mentally tough, and if you weren't you either figured out how to get mentally tough or you got out.
I only left because I wasn't going to be a ballerina. Because you either want that life or realize *No, I don't want that life.* I didn't want that life, I knew I was never going to be a ballerina because I didn't have that absolute desire to give up everything and all to have that kind of life.

CHAPTER 13

Doing work for the San Francisco Opera Ballet

According to both Dorothy and Tamara, their relationship began to become strained during Tamara's teenage years. Dorothy described their relationship as going from a mother/daughter one to a friendship in a way. This ultimately culminated in Tamara leaving at eighteen and disappearing from Dorothy's life, with nobody except Kimberli knowing Tamara's whereabouts. Dorothy blamed some of the breakdowns of their relationship on the overall culture shift in the late 60s and early 70s when this happened.

"...The whole country was going nuts and not realizing the damage it was doing to too many people," explained Dorothy.

This lasted for a while with both Dorothy and Jim not knowing where Tamara had gone.

"What bothered me the most was that Kimberli knew exactly where she was and didn't tell me. By this time, Kimberli had moved out with her boyfriend who later became her husband. Tamara had been gone, nobody told me where she was. Nobody told Jim where she was. You have any idea what it's like not to know where your daughter is? Then I got a call from Boston, Massachusetts…"

It was Tamara on the other end. Dorothy had found out that Tamara had moved to San Francisco to dance for the San Francisco Opera ballet and then eventually went on to dance in Boston.

This is where this part of Dorothy's story gets complicated. Dorothy explained, "I found out that she went to San Francisco with this young man who was from a big shot soccer family and danced with the Opera Association. The director and choreographer of the Opera Association was Norbert Vesak, a friend of mine, but he didn't know that she was my daughter."

But Tamara gives a different version of how she came to dance with the San Francisco Opera Association.

"The director of the Opera Ballet [Norbert] at that point was a person who had come to Dorothy's studio and choreographed a few ballets. So I auditioned, and he already knew me because he'd worked a little bit with me. That's how that came about. I had to audition because it was a union audition. Although I wasn't a member of the union everybody had to audition to see who wanted to be in those particular productions. So he took me," explained Tamara.

Tamara eventually made it back to California. One evening, Tamara randomly showed up at the home of her parents according to Dorothy.

"I got a knock on the door one evening. I opened up the door and this young man helps Tamara in, sick as a dog. I don't know how she got back to California but this young man brought her, a young boy. And I told him 'Don't you ever come down my street because I'll kill you.' I meant it. You see your daughter come in like that and be used and abused by some asshole. I'll never get over that, ever. And I meant it, I said 'If you ever walk down my street I'll kill you, so be careful.' His mommy and he lived two blocks down so I went to mommy's house and knocked on the door. I told her what her son had done and I told her I'd kill him if he came back near my house. That is the worst possible thing that could happen to a parent, worst possible thing. You see this beautiful girl; talented, smart, and being used and abused," Dorothy explained.

The emotions that Dorothy had from dealing with situations like this began to pour into her work in ballet.

"That's a part of my life that I can use when I do something in ballet, to know what it feels like, to know what the emotions are like. If it was a ballet that was about trauma, that had that feeling about it, I didn't have to make up those feelings. I didn't have to tell my students this is why I'm feeling this way, this is why I have to do this," said Dorothy.

It should be noted that this was all the information I was able to get out of Dorothy and her daughters about this situation since it was such a sensitve subject. A fear of mine throughout the process of writing this book was causing more turmoil in an already complex situation. On one hand I learned pretty early on that when it comes to journalism you're not doing it right unless someone is angry at you. But the last person I want to make angry is Dorothy because I don't know if I could handle getting the stink eye from that woman.

CHAPTER 14

Passing of Loved Ones

Dorothy's friendship had continued with Josephine throughout the 1960s and early 70s.

"When Tammy was in high school I was still visiting with her. Never once did she ask 'Do you want to join the church?' Never once, but she did ask me if I wanted to go to an Easter service with her one time and I said yes. Now, this has been years that she's been coming once a week, never once pushing her religion, such a nice, nice woman. So I said I would like to go to a Jehovah's Witness Easter. I wanted to see what it was like.

"So we went, there were forty to sixty people there. And the preacher says at the end of the service 'Those who feel worthy of sitting at the Lord's table and taking communion please come forward.'

"You couldn't have drug me out of my seat. One man, one grey-haired man walked up out of all the people that were there and took communion on eEaster. It left such an impression on my mind, it doesn't matter what church you want to put the title on, it's your relationship with the Supreme Being. That's why there was no way you could've gotten me up to take communion."

Despite the fact that Dorothy had very little time to socialize outside of ballet, time was always made for Josephine's visits. One of these visits in particular was very important.

"So, one day Josephine came to my house and she had a young woman with her."

Dorothy said that they all sat in the same space where I had interviewed her at the very moment, with Dorothy sitting one side of the area with Josephine and the other young woman sitting on the other side.

"There is this young woman, probably in her late 20s or 30s. And so we're studying something, some passage. And I said, "Well, I don't understand that, I don't get what you're saying." Just then the young woman interrupted "Well, that's really stupid. It's really clear."

Josephine, embarrassed, began apologizing to Dorothy.

Dorothy said very sternly, "Take her out of my house and don't ever bring her back again. Never.

I don't ever want that woman in my house again."

"Well, I've stayed too long with you. We're only supposed to stay a couple of weeks and this has been years," explained Josephine. Dorothy, saddened by this said "I understand, I'll miss you, but I understand."

This was the last time Dorothy would see Josephine, but she never forgot about her. And a few years later Dorothy ran into Josephine's daughter while walking down the street in Stockton.

"Oh, how's your mom?" asked Dorothy.

Her daughter then said solemnly, "Oh Dorothy, she died."

"She was dying?"

Dorothy then realized that was why Josephine couldn't come back for her weekly visits; Josephine was trying to find a replacement study partner for Dorothy before she passed on. Despite the religious differences between Dorothy and Josephine, the two women never let that get in the way of their friendship. "My dad, the best man I've ever known, was Church of Christ. The lady across the street is Latter Day Saints, a wonderful person. You're [the author] Catholic, you're a pretty neat guy, your parents are wonderful. So the title doesn't matter if it's one Supreme Being. And that's what I've tried to live by.

Around the same time of learning about Josephine's death, Dorothy lost her first dance partner: her father.

"Dad died at the hospital, he had a leg removed because he had cancer. And he said to me, "We can't go hunting anymore Dorothy." And I said, "Well, come on dad. We could make you a wheelchair to go hunting anytime you want."

He passed on with Dorothy by his side, but never lost his sense of humor. Of her parents Dorothy said "I honored them, I loved them very much. They moved Heaven and earth. They knew they had this weird child," chuckled Dorothy.

Dorothy at 10 years old in one of her dance costumes.
(Courtesy Photo/Dorothy Percival)

Dorothy (right) and her sister Billie in 1947.
(Courtesy Photo/Dorothy Percival)

Marietta (top left), Billie,
Dorothy, Ruby (bottom left),
and Dorothy's mom in the
late 1950s.
(Courtesy Photo/Dorothy Percival)

Tamara and Jim in 1953.
(Courtesy Photo/Dorothy Percival)

Dorothy's parents in 1953.
(Courtesy Photo/Dorothy Percival)

Dorothy at 17 posing in her
bathing suit.
(Courtesy Photo/Dorothy Percival)

Dorothy at her studio in March, 1973.
(Courtesy Photo/Dorothy Percival)

Dorothy posing in her garden in the mid 1960s.
(Courtesy Photo/Dorothy Percival)

In this photo, Dorothy Percival is seen in the role of Bernarda Alba, in the ballet *The House of Bernarda Alba*, performed in 1983. Dorothy Percival is the founder of the Professional Organization for Performing Artists (P.O.P.A.).

The House of Bernarda Alba is Federico Garcia's last play, written the year he was killed at the outbreak of the Spanish Civil War. The play, along with *Blood Wedding* and *Yerma*, forms a trilogy expressing what Lorca saw as the tragic life of Spanish women. It is a play expressing the costs of repressing the freedom of others. The setting is specific to the values and customs of a rural Spanish people, but the plot's appeal is universal rather than national.

P.O.P.A.
Professional Organization for Performing Artists / Ballet San Joaquin
Artistic Director: Dorothy Percival (209) 477-4141

XP Multimedia (209) 810-6654

Dorothy in her 30s.
(Courtesy Photo/Dorothy Percival)

One of Dorothy's dance lesson posters
circa 1947.
(Courtesy Photo/Dorothy Percival)

(Courtesy Photo/Dorothy Percival)

(Top & Bottom) Beth Main (white costume on the right) and other dancers during the production of *The House of Bernarda Alba* in the 1970s.
(Courtesy Photo/Dorothy Percival)

Dorothy in the 1960s.
(Courtesy Photo/Dorothy Percival)

Dorothy in the 1970s.
(Courtesy Photos/Dorothy Percival)

CHAPTER 15

Working with Joffrey Ballet

In the 1970s, Dorothy began working with famed ballet choreographer and Joffrey Ballet co-founder Robert Joffrey during her month-long trips to New York.

Like Norbert Vesak, Joffrey was a very well-known and influential figure in the ballet community. He had taught at the New York High School of Performing Arts before going on to found his own New York based school in 1953 called the Joffrey Ballet School. (There is also a Joffrey Ballet based in Chicago, but the two companies are not affiliated as most people think). Every year, Dorothy would take a pilgrimage to Joffrey Ballet School in order to practice and study. Joffrey's shows and reputation allowed him and his dancers to perform at illustrious locations like The White House; and global locations such as The Soviet Union during the Cold War, the Middle East, and even India. "I like how he did his stories. I liked his approach to ballet; it was not just ballet, he had meat in his stories. So I started going up at least once a year to study with his school. And he appreciated and respected my work. So much so that when the group had to be, and I can't remember the two women, but there were two other women that were picked to go pick the outstanding male dancer in the world and I was one of them." said Dorothy. This led to Dorothy and Joffrey not becoming friends per se like she was with Norbert Vesak, but respected colleagues. At some point Joffrey asked Dorothy to accompany him to Paris, France to choose the best dancer in the world.

Many of Dorothy's students began learning under the Joffrey Ballet due to her connections with the company. Terry, Beth, and Marcia recall their time with Joffrey.

TERRY PAGO

So when she took me under her wing I remember her taking me to Joffrey Ballet. I remember the first professional ballet I had seen was by Jerome Robbins, it was called *Moves*. In my mind, I thought *I can do this*. But I didn't think I could do that as a dancer, I thought I could do that as a choreographer. So along with my dancing, she would lay out little hints like "Oh would you ever want to start choreographing?" I had it in the back of my mind until suddenly she just sprung it on me and said "Why don't you choreograph something?" I was like *Okay*. So that's how it began, and with that she really promoted me and let me do anything I wanted to do. The thing about her is she had impeccable taste and what she would do is fix my work, or lead me and say "You know what? You might want to rethink this." In two or three years I had done some, I wouldn't say great work, I had done some good work. In Santa Barbara, I won an award that nobody else in my age category should have won; I had won best choreography at a festival, and that's when she

really started gearing me away from dancing towards choreography. It was good but it wasn't easy, it wasn't a fairy tale but
she got people to take me seriously because she had developed
me as a choreographer and a person. It helped me stand up for
myself and be a little more confident in life, which I was.

BETH MAIN

When I was 17 Dorothy got me a scholarship to the Joffrey Ballet here in New York City. And she got two other students in my
community at the time, Julia Armstrong, Stacy Sheffield, and
me, and Dorothy got each of us a scholarship. Julia and I got
one to the Joffrey and Stacy got one to the School of American
Ballet, the theater school for the New York City Ballet. And she
took us to New York City. This is 1975: she chaperoned us, we
spent a summer here. It was my introduction to New York City.
My dad supplemented the scholarships so that I took one class
in the morning at the Joffrey school and then because my father
was so generous, I was able to take two additional classes every
day at the American Ballet Theatre (ABT). So it was a really
intense summer.
And there was Dorothy, Dorothy would go. She couldn't see,
she couldn't be everywhere at once.
Stacy had the most potential at the time of the three of us. So
Dorothy went with Stacy to her classes, and she sat in them and
took notes. And then we'd all gather at the end of the day and
the little studio apartments in our pajamas. And Dorothy would
pull out the notes and there in our pajamas and our bare feet we
would do a bar based on the things that Dorothy wanted Stacey
to work on, we all worked on.

So it was Dorothy's intensity that was the reason that we even got to New York, to these schools. And she helped us get the most out of the experience because she was as intense as the schools themselves were intense. Because at that time, we were all considering careers as professional ballet dancers. And if you're not gonna excel, go home. Because there are a lot of others all around you who excel. So it was intimidating as all hell but also so exhilarating.

MARCIA HENDRICKS

So I think the next big plumb thing that Dorothy touched in my life was the summer before I went to my freshman year at UC Santa Barbara. She had reached out to me and invited me over. When we would go to the studio, if anybody else has talked to you about the studio that was in her home, we would come through a back gate and enter through a sliding glass door into a ground floor room where we could stretch and warm up and use the bathroom. And then you went upstairs into this upstairs studio.

We weren't going into her main home. I mean, you always smelled wonderful things that her husband was cooking for dinner. But we rarely went inside the main home. So she reached out to me and invited me over and had me come in the front door. And I think we had coffee or something. But her purpose of getting me there, and I'm sure she wanted to see me before I left for college too, but she had had this amazing experience that summer. Where a physical therapist and occupational therapist had reached out to her and had asked her as a dance professional to come be a special guest at a camp for physically handicapped children.

And she was so excited working with these therapists because she saw that dance teachers and therapists were trying to do the same thing. Organize people's bodies to be stronger, more mobile, have strength, core strength, control, all these things. And she just was like, Marsha, have you ever thought of being a physical therapist. So she was the one that planted in my brain to look into that further, which, during the rest of that summer, the Walton Education Center where I had been volunteering. And I knew the director of that school, she was the mother of a boy I dated earlier in high school. She was happy to connect me with the physical therapist that would come through. And that really pointed me in the direction of at first thinking that I wanted to be a pediatric physical therapist, and I pursued all the groundwork education at UC Santa Barbara to be able to apply to graduate school and I graduated.

I was successful in getting into the program at Stanford University's physical therapy program, their school of medicine. And in the process of going through that, and still pursuing maybe being a pediatric therapist. I had a real awakening when I had an internship at Oakland Children's Hospital, which was pretty intense.

CHAPTER 16

Dorothy's Rigorous Encouragement

Despite many of Dorothy's students moving on to careers outside of the world of dancing, her words continue to ring inside the minds of her students to this day. Many of them expressed how her "encouraging" approach and values are still something that they live by today.

BETH MAIN

You know, we've become such a flabby— I don't mean that literally, I mean metaphorically we become a flabby, self-indulgent, trivial culture— and Dorothy was none of that. If we came in and complained, she would sit our heads right back on our shoulders. "Your toes hurt? Let me see them." She would demand that we aspire to be noble, to be strong, to be poised, to be capable. Do it again, do it again, do it again. "That's not your best is it?" "I can't do it." "Yes, you can do it. You can do it. Here's what we're going to do. Since you're busy crying right now, you're going to come in tomorrow."

I got this once. I was rehearsing the pas de deux to *Don Quixote*, and the guy was named Rico Costa. Rico and I were rehearsing, it was an incredibly difficult ballet. I was 16, I think, and learning it was incredibly difficult. Way over my head, I go home every day and cry to my mom, "I can't do it, I can't do it! She thinks I'm better than I am!" And I would say that the opposite was true, that she saw only what I was capable of. She wouldn't ask me to do something she didn't know I couldn't get to. And she was there at my side to get me there, which turned out to be the case.

But I had a hard time and my ankles, my God, my ankles became... I had a lot of problems with my ankles. And so instead of feeling sorry for me, when I would collapse on the floor and say, "I just can't, I can't." She would say, "Okay, you can, and you will. And we're just going to do this until you can. And I want you to, starting tomorrow, I want you to come in by yourself 30 minutes before the scheduled class or rehearsal. And I want you to do relevés at the bar barefoot and start strengthening those ankles."

I don't know what we expected differently. But it was never "Oh, you poor thing. I guess you can't." She never gave up on us. Like she didn't give up on the San Joaquin Valley. She never gave up on us and it, and then we discovered what we were capable of.

MARCIA HENDRICKS

I really pondered before my senior year in high school whether I wanted to keep doing this. I felt like it was a lot of hard work and sacrifice. And I wondered if I was giving up a lot in high school. So I kind of had made a mental thought that I was not going to audition for my final year of youth ballet.

And of course, my original ballet teacher caught me somewhere in the community, I think the day before the audition, and she confronted me with it. She urged me strongly to stick with it, that she felt I did have things to offer the company. So I did, and I'm glad I did.

I kind of started to gain respect from Dorothy in that we had an experience where we traveled to learn choreography of a piece called *Simple Symphony*. It had a pas de deux [a dance for two people] in it and it had the core dancers, and I was part of a core. But a lot of the core work, again, was very specific on very specific counts, really emphasizing musicality. With my background of studying both piano and flute, I really knew music well and I knew counting well. I kind of have this almost photographic memory. And when we got back to the studio, and tried to recite it, a lot of people hadn't paid close attention to what they were supposed to be doing. And I started to speak up and she really tapped into the fact that I had got it. So I kind of helped everybody remember what we were supposed to be doing and when and where and how and what notes had been given. And so that gained a little respect or she saw that in me, which I appreciated.

So I felt that maybe I didn't have the perfect body, I was behind a little bit in my training, but I had something to offer and I think that was really good. She did know that I was not plan-ning to pursue dance and some of that was harpooned by my parents, even though I showed the potential and I was devel-oping nicely. Dorothy had recommended to my parents that I spend a summer program at the School of Fine Arts, which is what the upper division girls were doing at the time. And you know, my dad didn't support it, quite honestly, he was this depression era baby boy who just didn't see spending money on things that he thought might not buy us value in the future.

So I often never had that chance during the summer to train because Dorothy often traveled during the summer with dancers, so the studio was closed. So I would lose some conditioning and some progress that I had made.

So I kind of was expected by my parents [to attend college], and I had always been a super strong student. I applied to universities and I ended up committing and planning to go to UC Santa Barbara. And at the time, I thought I wanted to be a teacher like my mom, but maybe in special ed because I had had some experience in doing a teacher assistant stuff through high school in special ed.

CHAPTER 17

Cold War Era Ballet

The chaos in Dorothy's schedule never ceased to exist through all decades of her teaching. Dorothy would teach her classes during the day, and as soon as they were over, get in the car and head to whatever major company needed her. If she was lucky she'd grab a sandwich that she could eat while driving. But despite how hectic and time-consuming it all was, Dorothy said she loved every minute of it even if there were times "...when I'd be disgusted and angry with a director maybe because he didn't know as much as he should."

In 1980 during the Cold War, Dorothy traveled to Moscow and Leningrad as a seminar participant and observer of international ballet competitions. Things get a little bit hazy for Dorothy during this time especially when it comes to names, but one person she does remember traveling to the U.S.S.R with was Robert Joffrey. Robert would bring top dancers from his company to judge these competitions. Dorothy attended these competitions until 1983.

During this three-year stretch, she also traveled to Triblisia (Georgia) to practice the Vaganova Method of ballet, which

Dorothy described as six weeks of intensive study. From there she met many famous people from the ballet community including famed Russian choreographer/dancer Rudolf Nureyev who is often regarded as one of (if not the) greatest male dancers in classical ballet. He was known for how closely he would stick to classic ballet stemming from his perfectionist style much like Dorothy.

During these times when Dorothy would travel to the U.S.S.R., she would leave her best students in charge of her classes. The times in the U.S.S.R were filled with Dorothy forming connections with a variety of people. Some of these people were dancers who ended up traveling to the United States in order to participate in her shows.

TERRY PAGO

You have to consider this, she's [Dorothy] in a small town and there she is Dance in Stockton. So she had a lot of weight on her shoulders because she wanted all of her dancers to look good. And bless her heart, she always had people come in to choreograph ballets and to give us some kind of exposure. But when you're not in a large city and don't see what the competition is, you sort of get lax.

She could be funny at times, but some of the times were really, really miserable. And I remember she threw a chair at me rehearsing one ballet, I had obviously done something wrong in her eyes. But when it all came to an end, especially in the 70s and 80s, all was forgiven and we started over again. But some of the times were very, very intense.

Again, she had a really, really good eye and I'm glad she passed it on to all of her other instructors. You know she did really good when I was with the company. It was a very, very strong company. We had maybe five, you know, pre-professional dancers, where she could have turned it into a semi-professional company if we hadn't all gone. But for us, even though it was difficult there was always an aura of respect, even though there were difficult times for us as dancers.

There were so many difficult times there. But you know in her defense, when somebody gets that deep into their art they're not going to step aside. They're going to go straight through it. They're going to accomplish what they want to accomplish, no matter how many toes get stepped on.

You know, she took on, oh my God, she fought with everybody that got in her way. Some was very, very valid, like she fought with the union. Leo Berg had to have a union person doing lights for something he never rehearsed on but he had to be on the salary. The whole union stuff, which I really didn't understand for Stockton, I really can't speak to it.

I remember drinking a lot of coffee with her and smoking a lot of cigarettes and staying in the house until 1:00 in the morning. And we would chit chat, we were friends.

The thing about Dorothy Percival is it was compartmentalized, there was this time for fun where she could just be with us, there was a classroom situation where she was basically very supportive and was a fine teacher. And then there was the time with a company that got a little crazy. There are many layers to Madam Percival. But that was one of our fun times.

I mean, she introduced me to New York. Before meeting her
I don't think I've ever been in a restaurant. I was a child from
the South Side and my family really didn't have money. And so
she actually did do a lot of exposure to the world which was a
stimulation for me to read a bit more and to look at things in a
different light. I'm a fan, I really am a fan of hers even though I
haven't seen her in a couple of years. Prior to that, I hadn't seen
her for some amount of years. I owe her so much, I really need
to see her.

I would probably be dead if it had not been for being scared
to death of Dorothy Percival. I was frightened of her in some
ways, I don't know if that's such a good thing. But my life could
have taken a twist for the worse. I became so codependent on
Dorothy creative-wise that when I flew the nest, my work was
just mediocre. I'm sorry that I flew last semester and I didn't
come back to better prepare myself for the field that I thought I
wanted to go with.

But, one thing she understood is that a lot of ballet directors
don't understand the creative process so she knew my flaws,
like I was dyslexic and I wasn't the best, I was reading words
backwards. With her, I was charged to do better and she got
it because dyslexic people have a tendency to be very focused
and are very creative. They don't see things literally as described to me by a shrink. Everything is not in line, but it's
circular. So my learning process is different and I just think she
honed in on that.

CHAPTER 18

Charter member of the Pacific Northwest Regional Ballet Association

On the national level for ballet, there are five regions across the United States. Dorothy, being from California, landed in the Pacific Northwest Regional Ballet Association. In order to qualify for this ballet association, a ballet company would have to put forth two to three dancers for an audition. To top that off, you had to be one out of three companies on Gala Nights, which is the night of the Gala that only showcases the best of the best. You would present your company to a panel of three judges. All the instructors ranged from all over the United States, from Los Angeles to New York.

After the dancers were chosen, their respective companies were tasked with putting on a show, or workshop, on a different night over the course of two to three days. So these festivals were, and still are, a pretty big deal in the ballet community. Dorothy's company Ballet San Joaquin – was chosen every single year. Not only was Ballet San Joaquin chosen every year, but they were also the highest scoring company, constantly raking in ten out of ten scores.

As Dorothy explained this to me her bitterness towards the city of Stockton, where Ballet San Joaquin was based, came through. "The city of Stockton had their head that far up their ass, no idea what they had here. I always say I can bend this way and this way and this way and this way..." Dorothy then leaned forward and made the "kissing ass" gesture. "...but I have never accomplished that way. I cannot kiss ass, I cannot. People would say you have to learn how to do that Dorothy but I said no, uh uh, I could not live with myself. If I'm not good enough with what I present, then I don't want it. I don't want to be made a fool of on stage. But remember, ten out of ten..."

Kimberli, Elizabeth, and Melissa recalled how it was at the company during this time period.

KIMBERLI CAMPBELL

I can't tell you years but she's probably brought it up where she had a regional company status. We were dancing, maybe I was 13, 14, 15 somewhere in there. Then she started into *The Nutcracker* productions which became pretty intense. She's always been very passionate and very intensely proud of everything that she has done and trying to get things perfect. That's always been her whole mark I think.

ELIZABETH ARCHER

We used to attend the Pacific Northwest Regional conference and that was amazing. Nowadays, it's called Regional Dance America, RDA. It's so— and I don't even know if they're still doing it, to be honest with you. I did actually take some of my dancers to one of the Pacific Northwest Regional conferences a while back, probably 10 years ago. It was such an amazing experience to participate with youth dance companies from across the region. So all the way from Washington down into Arizona was that particular conference.

You got to take classes with master teachers, including people like Robert Joffrey. One of my dancers actually went on to dance with Joffrey professionally. You would get to take these classes, not just ballet, but different genres and disciplines.

You'd get to see amazing, amazing talent, and award-winning dance companies and work that they did. The work that we got to do, that we got to bring to concert-based competition didn't really feel like competition in those days thank God because I'm not a fan of competition at all.

I'm really grateful that [Dorothy] taught us the difference between competitive dance and concert-based dance because it honors the art form so differently and I can't even imagine being judged for something that I love doing so deeply. I don't get the mindset behind competition so our studio is not a competitive studio. But the festival provided us the opportunity to make contact with other dancers from other regions. Like I said, just amazing, beautiful artistry, technical. And the cool thing was that, while it wasn't competitive, depending on your abilities, your technical background, the type of creative work you were presenting, you could work your way up to become a performing member or a charter member. And it was really an amazing thing to strive for because we wanted to be in that top tier, especially from that creative and technical perspective. It was just a really, really fine memory and a really great experience.

I know part of her legacy is that I wanted to share this and extend this to not only my own training but my dancers. They have had the opportunity to work with world-class dancers, world-class choreographers, gone on two world-class companies, and she's the seed that planted that.

MELISSA ESAU

Back in the 60s and 70s— and they don't have these anymore, at least I don't think they have them anymore— if they do, they're different. But they used to have regional dance festivals and ours was the Pacific Regional Dance Festival. You would have three days and it would be hosted in a city that would be able to hold hundreds of people, not only spectators but dancers. They would have to put you up in hotels— that's when you would use the big ballrooms at these big hotels. They would invite guest teachers in from all over the United States to give you master classes in ballet, in jazz, not tap, but character, and maybe a pas de deux class. You would be working with all of these great instructors of the time.

And prior to these festivals, which are usually in April, May something like that, you would be working on ballets. And you would present two or three ballets. So there would be an adjudicator that would come who was another big name in ballet and look at them, watch them, give critique, and say, *Okay, on this ballet that you just did, would I want it to be on the Gala night,* which was the big night. The first two nights were good, but you always wanted to be at the Gala. The best companies were always at the Gala and as far as I can remember the five years we went we were always at the Gala.

Really that was a tribute to the fact of how we were trained, it was professional in capital letters, exclamation point. So because of that, we got to go to different places. We would go to Southern California, we went up to Washington or we would go to wherever the regional festival was, we would get to go there. And so we got a lot of great experiences, we got to work with a lot of great instructors, ballet masters, who we might not have gotten to work with at like 13 years old. Now, these names might not mean anything to you but at the time it was Michael Sims, David Howard, Maria Tallchief. I mean, there were all of these people, Sally Bliss, Henry Berg from the Joffrey, there were a lot of big names that would come and give master classes.

And out of these classes, and these performances, you could be offered scholarships to go to dance at a company for the summer. One year we did Several Songs, which was a Norbert Vesak ballet and we performed it at Gala. And one of the directors, I think it was Richard Gibson from San Francisco Ballet who said, "Any of your girls could have a scholarship to San Francisco Ballet just by watching this ballet." So those kinds of good things that came out of these Gala performances were great. We just never would have gotten those things if we were with another dance studio.

One of the reasons that Norbert Vesak liked to work with Dorothy and choreographed a lot of ballets for her is because she would sit and watch him choreograph. And she would listen to all of the words that he used. If you were a company and you wanted a Norbert Vesak ballet he most likely would have

charged you. I remember her saying he never charged her for
any of these ballets.

So she listened to the words that he would use and use those
words when cleaning up the ballet and working with us. So
when he would come back to either watch it or add more to it,
he'd be like, "Oh my gosh, this is really good. You guys have
worked hard and you're getting it." So he really liked Dorothy
and he liked working with her. He appreciated the fact that she
was going to take care of his ballets and do them justice the
way that he envisioned them to be done. She was super, super
good with that.

One year we did a whole night. That's how many ballets she
had. We did a whole night of Norbert Vesak ballet and *Gift
to be Simple* which is that three minutes that we spent four
hours on, that was a Norbert Vesak ballet. And God we did a
whole night of his work because that's how many pieces he had
done. And I was lucky enough that there were two ballets that I
actually got to learn from him because he choreographed them
just for Dorothy's girls. One of them was *Several Songs* and the
other one was called *Bridle Path* that he did specifically for our
company. The other ballets he had done for other companies
that he just recreated for us, but I was lucky enough to learn two
original ballets of his. And that was kind of fun but it was still
really hard, you had to be smart. And that was another thing I
learned from Dorothy— which I think all of us did and all of
us have utilized it throughout our life— is you got to be a quick
learner. You have to be able to see something once or twice, be
able to execute it, and remember it because you're going to add
on to it. So you had to have a great memory, and you had to

learn something really quick. Nothing agitated her more if you couldn't remember, like something that was given two minutes ago, you better remember it, and get it and keep it and move on. So you had to be a fast learner and that's something that has stayed with me this whole time. You pick things up, you learn because I did a lot of theatre after I left her. So I learned choreography really easily. I learned my lines really easy because you don't get to go back and do it again. You have to learn it and move on and keep going- and you better remember it or else.

I really wanted to find a paper trail for all of these organizations that Dorothy said that she was a part of, not that I didn't believe her. While over at her house she let me look through her library which contained archives upon archives of her past career. From home movies, photographs, scripts, and paperwork, it was all there. While she was rummaging through the memories of her long career Dorothy found exactly what I was looking for. "I ran across some papers where I was investigated to belong to the regional association. I didn't realize I was so good. I love that paper." chuckled Dorothy.

The paper she had found was dated from 1985, so it was after the events that Elizabeth and Melissa had told me about. But the document was fascinating as it really showed a window into Dorothy's teaching method through the eyes of another professional. Here are some excerpts:

VISITATION REPORT

Date of Visitation: April 27, 1985

Time of Visit: 9:45 to 10:45 A.M.

School Visited: American Dancin' Drama Inc.

Class Visited: Ballet

Report of What Was Observed.

This class follows the same format as all the classes at this school. The instructor leads the class in stretch exercises while doing them with the class. These stretches are specifically geared to each age group. She corrects and guides each student as they move through the exercises. She uses positive reinforcement in the important areas. Keep the legs straight (when they are supposed to be); point the toes; make sure the knees are aligned with the toes; keep the head up and the back straight with the tail-bone down. In ballet, there are many things to concentrate on at the same time. Of course, with the younger students, the attention span is shorter, but this instructor has a lot of patience. She also uses comparisons, likening correct posture to a toaster. If the student does not keep a straight body, they will get burned from the red hot walls in front and behind. She also used "table legs", meaning if the leg that the student is standing on is not kept straight then the table, and student will fall. I think at the same time the student is helped by the mental image it creates.

When a student does something well, the teacher will ask her to demonstrate it for the class. When someone has a specific problem, the entire class will observe them and try to analyze it.

The class works on a sequence of steps and then concentrates on those that give them problems. Here the instructor leads the class through the exercise, making corrections as necessary. Different sequences were handled in this manner. At the same time, the class is learning about rhythm and counting steps to the beat. In ballet there are many, many things to concentrate on.
Ballet teaches children discipline, muscle control, and body placement.

<u>*What I Liked.*</u>
I feel that the students learn a great deal from their instructor. She watches her pupils as a group and also as individuals. The teacher herself is with them, guiding them for the entire hour. She does not allow the students to fool around. She disciplines them with a gentle hand.

The class also rehearses the routine they will perform. At this time, the instructor works intensely with her class, leading them through it. The teacher literally runs to each side of the room so that she can be in front of the class coaching them at the same time. She corrected errors and gave a lot of encouragement.

I think that all the children felt themselves part of the group, nor did they hesitate to point out to the teacher when believed that she made a mistake. This showed me that all her students are comfortable and honest with her.

What I Would change or Handle Differently.

I can not think of anything that I would do differently. The instructor had limitless patience. She observed, corrected, and guided her students to the best of their ability. She handled them firmly but kindly using humor to keep those little mind's attention. She consistently reinforces the importance I think that this is very important because points of dance, teachers are role models for children.

Would I Like to Teach This Subject.

Yes, I would like to teach this subject at this level, but as I have said before, only if I felt qualified to do so. I shall elaborate further on this, I have studied a particular dance form for nine years and performed it in public for over half of those years. I know what my level of teaching ability was after three years of study and I believe that only after many years of study is some-one qualified to teach others. I think that if I were teaching and I became aware that I was inadequate for the job, then I would stop teaching. I know from personal experience as a student, that it is very hard to correct wrongly taught dance technique.

VISITATION REPORT

Date of Visitation: April 30, 1985
Time of Visit: 3:45 to 4:45 P.M.
School Visited: American Dancin' Drama Inc.
Class Visited: Tap Dance

Report What I Observed.
The same basic format is followed with this class, which is stretching, bar exercise, center floor work, and movement across the floor.

As I watched her teach, I realized very quickly that she has limitless patience. She was good at keeping the class moving along. At the same time, she would correct errors and instruct her pupils. She started her class at the bar with exercises to stretch the feet and ankles. This warm-up prepares them for dancing. At this time her students go through a series of steps and the teacher observes and corrects errors.

In tap dancing it is important to keep the feet directly under the body, however, I did notice that the pupils have the tendency to step too far forward, thus losing the sharpness of the tap. The teacher continually reminds her class to keep their heads up (it does not help the feet to watch them), and the knees bent. It seems to me that the noise level could drive you crazy, but this teacher kept her class moving along at a steady pace without hesitations nor many problems. At one point she did stop the class so that she could work with each individual.

What I Liked.
I believe that it is good for the student to learn the importance of stretching and warming up before dancing. This prevents injuries although they are less likely to occur in tap dance. I

agree with the teacher's method of instruction, that is to keep
the class fast-paced. This keeps the interest of the student.
She gives them a lot of material to learn and they continually
work on polishing their technique. As she pointed out, tap is
not as disciplined as ballet, but ballet is a good beginning for
any dancer.

I noticed that she consistently corrected difficulties in a positive
manner, giving her pupils verbal support. Here she urged the
students to accompany themselves verbally. Also, the students
learn to work together as a group, which is an important experience for children.

What I Would Change or Handle Differently.

I do not think that I would change or handle anything differently. This teacher obviously has years of training and teaching
experience. I totally agree with having a set format for dance
instruction. I also would not slow the pace of the class because I
understand the importance of keeping the students interested.
Would I Like to Teach this Subject.

Tap dancing is a fun style of dance, more relaxed in discipline
than others I would be interested in teaching this style of dance
at this level. However, I would not do so unless I had training
and experience myself. Handling youngsters would be a great
challenge and I am not sure if I possess the patience of this instructor. This will be the only area that I am unsure about.

VISITATION REPORT

Date of Visitation: May 4, 1985
Time of Visit: 9:00 to 12:00 A.M.
School Visited: S.J.D.C.
Class Visited: Modern Dance

Report of What Was Observed.

These classes are for beginners through advanced. The instructor leaves a blank piece of paper to be used for roll-call. She expects her students to sign themselves in. She then called her T.A.'s to the front of class to lead. At this point, a girl came in with a big tray of food and drink for the instructor (and others), who slipped out not to return for 45 minutes. When she did come back in, she sat by the phonograph to restart the music whenever necessary.

She began to instruct the advanced class as they worked on a new routine. The T.A. leading the class became frustrated with the beginners and left them to work with the advanced group. So
the beginners stood there with no one in charge. I also heard the instructor say "I'm learning this routine along with you! Ha, ha!"

What I Liked.

There is little that I can cite other than the dance routine itself was good. However, it was suited for advanced students.

What I Would change or Handle Differently.

First of all, I would take a verbal roll-call in order to become acquainted with my students. Next, I would teach beginning students fundamentals of the dance form which I instruct. I would have a teaching outline for my class. I believe in continual repetition in order to teach the basics of dance. All students need a good foundation upon which to build and develop their own creativity. I would also stress the importance music has in dance, teaching rhythms, and counting. I would take time for "stretching" and "warm-ups" because I know that most inexperienced dancers do not take the time to do this on their own. Last but not least, I would develop a routine that would incorporate what they have learned. Also, I would teach dances by the level of experience, and learn them myself first.

<u>Would I Like to Teach This Subject.</u>
Yes I would, however as I have stated before I would teach this subject when I believed I had received enough training, and had something to offer the students. This particular teacher can harm a student by her method. On the other hand, my observations have made me realize many things to avoid when I begin to teach.

I think that the self-expression of modern dance style can be either a hindrance or an advantage depending on the instructor. If I were teaching such a class, I would use the self-expression of the dance to allow students to develop their ability and style.

VISITATION REPORT

Date of Visitation: March 7, 1985
Time of Visit: 5:45 to 8:45 P.M.
School Visited: American Dancin' Drama Inc.
Class Visited: Ballet Program I, Program II, Program III.

Report What I Observed.

One class I observed was Program I, which is for selected first-time students, ages 5 to 6; another was Program II, which is the next step up and by invitation only. The last class was Program III, which is the school's dance company class.

As with all of the other classes I observed at this school, the outline is the same. That is, the class begins with stretches, then moves to bar work, and then on to the center floor.

The class moved to the bar and the teacher checks her students for proper placement, posture, etc. She verbally coaches them as they go through the exercises. "Keep your tail-bone down; make sure all your toes are on the floor." After the exercise she asks her class "Where were they?" Were they thinking about homework, or were they "here" in class. With her many years of experience, the teacher could see who was concentrating and who was not. At this time she points out to her class that it is better for them to be honest because they only hurt themselves if they are not.

The instructor consistently and continually corrects and re-minds her class of the various points they need to remember I noticed that her class is comfortable in asking questions about particular movements they do not understand or when they are having difficulties with a step.

Discipline is very important and the teacher proves this to the class by showing them their responsibility for self-discipline. She does it by asking her class if they are doing their own work or someone elses. The student who follows another who is not doing the sequence correctly is worse off than if they made their own mistakes.

When the class began to work on a new sequence of steps, the instructor would concentrate on getting the movement correct with the music, which is timing. She points out the relation of the flute in the music to the move they are studying. The instructor helps her students think through their problems by asking them questions. Such as "What is different about what we are doing?"
The students found the solutions to their problems in their answers. They discovered that the problem was the speed of the music.

In her more advanced classes, not as much correction is needed because the class knows terms and rhythms. The music used is played faster. The Program II class analyzes the aches of the feet and discusses "point". The class tries it, then one student is selected to demonstrate it. They become more aware of "self" and also pay attention to what is being discussed. At the end of the Program I and II classes, I was allowed to ask the students questions I wanted to know if the students perceived their teacher's strict discipline as being mean. After they thought about it, several raised their hands and said that they felt that she was "firm" or "strict" but never mean.

Other comments were that some students from other schools were never corrected on movements, but now they feel that they are being taught correctly. I was truly impressed with the intelligence of these young people.

What I Liked.

I was impressed with the capability of the instructor. It seems to me that she has the capability to motivate her stuäents. As I observed the class, I could see the intense concentration on the faces of her pupils. Considering her competency in ballet, I believe that she is justified in selecting qualified students for her programs. Rightfully so, her students should be intelligent and possess the sincere desire to learn. She is an outstanding teacher because of her knowledge of the dance and years of experience in ballet.

What Would I Change or Handle Differently.

There is absolutely nothing that I can think of that I might change. This instructor is by far the best I have studied with and/or observed.

Would I Like to Teach this Subject.

I never could achieve what this instructor has in teaching ballet. Ballet is a difficult and demanding dance form. I believe after observing this class that I could never meet the standard of this instructor. It would take years of study to approach her qualifications and talent.

She believes in her method of teaching, and the students must also share her view for her classes are always full, she demands a lot of her students, and they reap the fruits of her knowledge and expertise.

Good experiences & Analyses

50/50

CHAPTER 19

Departing from Dorothy

1985 was not only a pivotal year for Dorothy, but it was for one of her students as well. That year, Beth found herself at a difficult crossroads where many other dancers have found themselves. Do you continue dancing or move on to focus on other things?

BETH MAIN

So dad sat me down and unexpectedly said, "So what do you want to do? This is your last year of high school. You got one year, what do you want to do?" I was so surprised he asked me that. So I said, "I want to dance." And he said, "You know, I've been thinking about this, and your mom and I are incredibly proud of you. You have had an experience that very few people at your age had. And you've taken it so far and Dorothy's been such a gift. This is an incredible experience, but it's been a very narrow experience. You know you don't eat enough. You're at it seven days a week. You didn't go to proms, you didn't go to football games. You don't have a boyfriend, it's too disciplined. And I'm not gonna let you make a decision that's going to affect the rest of your life before you've had some experience of more of life. So here's the deal, you're going to go to college for one year. I don't care where you go. But you're going to go to college for one year. If after one year, you tell me you still want to dance I will support you. But you don't know what you're talking about right now and I can't let that happen." I was mortified and I remember that with my dad you didn't say no to my dad. So it never occurred to me to say no.

It took me months to tell Dorothy, took me months, I couldn't face it. Here's this woman who invested so much in me, I get emotional thinking about it and about her. I couldn't talk to her. So I handled it so poorly- I did leave and I don't actually remember the details. It's probably because it was so traumatic I blocked it out.

But she told me later, we recently met in New York about five years ago, she was here for the summer. I brought this up and I told her that I wish I had handled it with more maturity, but I wasn't mature. And she said, "You told me at the time that your father said that you weren't any good, or I wasn't good for you or something like that." I said, "I hope I never said that." I'll never know. I'll never know whether she misremembers it or I do. But we corrected the record. So all that to say, I went to college. And my dad is a smart man, and I loved college. I loved university life.

I want to take a moment to mention that Beth's father Harold was a lawyer who had handled a lot of legal things for Dorothy. I had tried to get an interview with Harold, who is in his late

90's at this point, but he declined on confidentiality grounds, something which I had to respect.

It is also worth noting some of the parallels between Dorothy leaving her teacher Elva Eilers and Beth parting ways with Dorothy. While working on this story and listening to the students you begin to see the impact Dorothy had on their lives. In some cases, she became more of a parental figure to her students than their own biological parents.

CHAPTER 20

A Mother/ Daughter team

As the years went on, Tamara became more and more involved in her mother's company, teaching classes such as contemporary ballet, beginners, and advanced. Many students pointed out the difference between Tamara and Dorothy's styles with Tamara leaning more towards a Russian style of ballet while Dorothy taught with French dancing principals.

TAMARA WAGNER
It went smoothly, it went okay, for a long time until I got to be, like, over 40 or so. And then there were some things that I would like to have seen changed and [Dorothy] wanted things to stay the way they were. Mostly, I did whatever she wanted me to do and taught what she wanted me to teach. And we had some problems when I started wanting to teach more contemporary and she wouldn't give me time in the schedule. I wanted to branch off into that more, while I was still into it but it didn't happen for quite a while. Eventually, she saw that people liked it and the attendance was good in the classes. So she started letting me teach my own contemporary class, by having more

time, I mean. I would only be given like half an hour or something at the end of our class. I didn't like the setup because I couldn't really teach anything, couldn't get anything done. But as she got older, she kind of went along with the flow of the move towards contemporary and ballet and all of that. So she saw the value of it, people liked it and I enjoyed doing that. So I think we probably started kind of working toward a little bit more of an equal basis around that point. Again, I went for years just doing exactly what she wanted me to do as long as I was available. It was not like she told me I had to, I wanted to do it.

Most of the time my relationship with the students was pretty good. There was a student who was just really disrespectful to me. When they work for me, or didn't, they didn't treat me like I had as much authority as Dorothy did. Most of the time, the kids would not work as hard for me in classes, as they worked for Dorothy. And while I understood that it got really old after a while, some people pushed it more than others. So that would make me not so nice at times. But for the most part, even my mother says I'm a nicer person than she is. That's the different personality type. I'm not as into myself as my mother is into herself. So I could always have a little bit too much empathy I think.

Sometimes you have to lay down the rules, lay down the law, and not get upset if somebody cries in your classroom or they can't get it right. Yeah, I got a little bit better with that as I got older. But still, that's just not me, I don't like to do intimidation.

Present 2000's until now

CHAPTER 21

Awards and loses

While doing research on Dorothy, an article popped up from the "Stockton Record" newspaper titled "Ballet San Joaquin founder earns honor for pursuit of excellence" which was written by Journalist Howard Lachtman. The article, published in October of 2000, was written about an award that Dorothy was receiving in the coming days called the STAR (Stockton Top Arts Recognition Award). This ceremony was taking place just two months shy of Dorothy and Jim's 51st wedding anniversary and included many of her former students.

"Dorothy Percival is committed to excellence in dance," read the article.

She wants students to leave her studio with the best possible preparation. In fact, she demands it. Which is why she's gained a reputation as a tough taskmaster. "I'm easy to get along with if you do what I ask," said Percival, founder and artistic director of Ballet San Joaquin. "When students

walk through my door, I tell them they are potential pro-
fessionals. My job is to prepare them with the skills they'll
need to make intelligent decisions about their careers." To
her admirers, Percival is the force who has kept ballet on
center stage in San Joaquin County for five decades and
linked Stockton to the ballet world. She has brought guest
artists to the community from the Joffrey Ballet, Paris Opera Ballet, American Ballet Theater, and The Bolshoi Ballet,
and her annual production of 'The Nutcracker' is a local
cultural highlight.

The article mentions the many professional dancers that she
would bring in for her yearly *Nutcracker* show, highlighting that
Dorothy has been the pipeline for much of the arts in the area.
The article continued:

"Dorothy is a perfectionist, and I love that about her," said
David Nelson, a Percival student and "Nutcracker" dancer
who'll present the award to his former teacher. "Because
what she did was to force us (her students) to be better than
we thought we could be. Everybody has a preconceived notion of what they can and can't do. She'd make you break
that notion and strive for the highest you could do, even
when you thought there was no way you could do it."

"All of her life, Dorothy has been tightly focused on her ballet company in its various incarnations," said Vince Perrin,
executive director of the commission. "Just to keep it going,
she fights against great odds, often at temperamental odds
with those who don't share her tunnel vision. While always
politically correct, she's not always politically polite."

"Dorothy is known as a difficult woman, which is another way of saying she did it on her own and made it on her own," said Stockton resident Christine Gray, former director of the Gender Studies Program at University of the Pacific who helped Percival with the preparation of her memoirs. "I think it's fabulous that she's a difficult woman. That's what makes her so interesting."

If Percival is tenacious and outspoken, it's in defense of a classical art form she says is under siege -- in Stockton and other communities throughout the country -- from the lack of funding and reduced standards.

The article wrapped by saying:

Still, [Dorothy] said, "When you do an art form, you work at it full-time, full-force. The important thing is the product that is on the stage, and it should be the best possible product. I have an obligation to the children who really want to dance, to their parents, to the public and to the art. It's not about me. I don't have that problem with my ego."

Percival admitted she is relentless, that she sometimes has to raise her voice at times 'and almost scream' to make some of her students get the point.

"They may think it harsh; but in the long run, it is filled with love," she said. Nelson, who now teaches English and speech at Stockton's Edison High School, said he had his own moments of doubt whether he could live up to Percival's constant demands. "Those who were strong would dig down and pull it out, and it was because of her," he said. Later, when Nelson heard an audience applauding, he said, "I knew I would not be there if it were not for Dorothy."

Many Percival students -- among them Nancy Memory (San Joaquin Delta College teacher and choreographer), Elaine Orimo-Dart (owner of Stockton Ballet School), Elizabeth Agardy (owner of The Dance Connection), Ricardo "Rico" Costa (a soloist with the Metropolitan Opera Ballet for 20 years and now a teacher at New York University and Peri Dance Studio), Alexander Goonan (who dances as Joseph Alexander with the MorganScott Ballet Company in New York), Greg Schanuel (Broadway dancer and national touring artist), Melissa Esau (Stockton Civic Theater actress, dancer and singer), Tricia Sundbeck (Sacramento Ballet principal), Beth Alley Archer (dance school and ballet company in Truckee) -- have gone on to successful careers in performance, choreography, and teaching. Percival said she takes pride in the award, "Especially on behalf of those who struggled to get it for me."

She said she'll continue her efforts to seek city funding to turn her organization into a professional company, so young dancers can stay here to learn the art. "I have gone this far without financial support from the city and I'm not quitting," Percival said. "My dream of a professional company hasn't stopped yet because I'm still breathing. The dream is still there."

In December of 2001, Jim passed on from heart problems after 52 years of marriage to Dorothy. She truly lost her partner in crime- all of the struggles and problems they had during their relationship washed away as Dorothy only remembers the good times.

Her house has many sections that are almost like museum pieces dedicated to Jim. His many paintings and woodworking pieces can all be seen around the house. In her basement, there are tables that have miniature wooden cabinets that look like something you would put in a dollhouse. The craftsmanship behind these pieces made me think they were done profession- ally, but no, they were done by Jim. To tie it all up, Dorothy has a glass-head mannequin set on a basement table with a white sweat-stained cowboy hat on it, a hat that you can tell has been through a lot. Dorothy explained that the battered hat was Jim's favorite, and she often imagines the mannequin wearing Jim's hat as a comforting presence, watching over everything in her home. Looking back through Dorothy's career and the rela- tionship she and Jim had, they really were the perfect union, a couple that was truly ahead of their time.

TAMARA WAGNER

I think they're a little better. I think after my father died and she didn't just have him always in her corner saying whatever she said she kind of lightened up a little bit. She realized, 'Well, maybe I better be a little nicer.' That's what he told her any- way right before he died. He asked her to be nice to me so that should tell you something about our relationship. I think my mother and I have pretty different personalities. We have some of the same talents but we're very different people inside, I'm way more sensitive than she is. I think there was a personality clash- there was just a lot of stuff that I couldn't handle. I once read an article that had to do with sports, it was addressing how hard it is for children, young teenagers, and younger kids to get pushed so hard and having so much demanded of them. And that if the line of communication isn't open then anxiety starts showing itself and if it's not acknowledged and you're not allowed to express your feelings then things get really rough. And you end up with problems, anxiety, and anxiety disorders- and I have them. In those days, people didn't pay that much attention to it really. I mean you're [Dorothy] having some success partially due to your child, and this was even harder because she was my mother and the company director. She couldn't see the signs I guess and it messed me up for a long time. But I think that's gotten better. I have gotten better, let me put it that way. So I can handle her more easily now than I could before.

CHAPTER 22

Dorothy "The Bitch" Percival

D orothy retired from her teaching position at Delta college in the mid 2000s. Dorothy was very proud of the reasoning behind her retirement because "I retired, not because I was kicked out but because I was so busy with the regional company that I didn't have time to do everything."

Dorothy recounted her early years at Delta, as well as a board member named Al Delorenga who she has fond memories of. Delorenga lived out in a farm town just outside of Stockton called Linden; Dorothy described Delorenga as "...just the nicest man." He built Dorothy ballet barres out of some disk plows, wood, and metal bars that he had on his property. He gave them to Dorothy when she started teaching at Delta in order to use them in her classroom.

"I used them at Delta because I didn't need them at the other places." explained Dorothy.

She ended up leaving them at Delta when she retired for the next instructor to use because they were not needed at her own studio.

Skip to 2019, the year I started writing this book, and Dorothy had just moved into a new studio. This studio needed ballet barres because it did not have any built into the walls like her previous studio spaces. So she decided to go back to Delta to get her bars that she had left behind.

"So I went to Delta college to get my barres because all these years they have been using them or not using them. And by the time I had left there, they had built barres into the wall so the only time we needed them was when we had a crowded classroom. Now mind you, I loaned the barres to the college. So a couple of months ago I wanted to use my ballet barres for my new place. So I went there and nobody could get my barres unless I talked to the teacher who teaches the class. And I said Valery, she teaches modern dance, there's ballet barres on the wall now, and I said I loaned these to you years ago and besides that they're mine. They were made by Al Delorenga for me. Couldn't do it, so I went back again to try and talk to somebody higher up and they said 'oh we can't do that, it wasn't done in writing.'" explained Dorothy.

She then raises her hand above her head, it is at this point that I can see the temper of Dorothy that so many feared.

"I tell you, I am up to here with piss. I'm just pissed. So I'm waiting to try and calm down a little bit and then have a meeting with the board of supervisors. I'm going to go in front of the board of supervisors and try to be kind. It's ridiculous, they have ballet barres in there now, why the hell should I have to talk to the damn teacher to get them back? I left four calls on her private phone and she has not returned one. I thought who in the hell do you think you are? She is a good modern dance

teacher but so am I. I'm a fantastic ballet teacher and I've got
a heck of a lot more years on her and have not a lot more than
just teach at Delta College. So I've tried to calm down."
Dorothy then chuckled.
"But then again, what can they do to me? I just go in and cuss
them out. Can they do anything to me? Nah, and make sure you
put that in the book."
Dorothy's frustration melted away as she laughed in her chair.

ADRIAN JUNEZ *was Dorothy's student from 2000 to 2016.*
I came to meet Dorothy in the year 2000. I met her at Delta
College, I actually signed up for her class. My feelings when I
first entered her class was a mixture of fright, happiness, anxiety, thrill— it was a mixture of everything. Because I had only
seen ballet schools in books and movies.
But to me, it seemed like one of those Monet paintings, the famous Monet paintings where you capture those moments of the
ballerinas where they're just stretching or talking or they're getting ready for class. That's how I felt, you came to this class and
you saw all these bodies moving in this beautiful uniform pace,
getting ready stretching in it, it looked like a movie. I felt like I
was in a movie or in a novel that I had just become a character
in. I never wanted to leave it, it felt wonderful, it felt exhilarating. I was breathing their same air, I know it sounds corny, but
it felt to me that way at that moment. I was just very happy to be
there, nervous, but happy.
I started my first class on a Tuesday morning at 7:30. This is
when I was 18 and I was taking public transportation. It was
a full class. There was about maybe 80 students and you saw

this dainty woman in her 60s around that time, she came up and she was dressed very spiffy, very nicely. She introduced herself by saying, "Good morning class. I am Dorothy 'The Bitch' Percival." Well of course seeing a woman in her 60s say that shocked me. But from there on I've known her now for 21 years. I have known her from 18 till 39.

So I have to go back to the beginning of my friendship with Dorothy. Back in 2000 when I was taking her class at Delta, we were learning how to waltz across the floor. We were learning you know chest up, long back, long neck, stomach in, and the proper etiquette for how to waltz in ballet. And I think I wasn't doing it correctly. Around that time I was wearing a V-neck Hanes shirt, a white one. I remember she came up to me, and I have hair on my chest, and she grabbed my chest, and I think accidentally, pulled the hairs from my chest. In that moment, I slapped her hand so hard. Everything was silent. I started apologizing profusely and that's when we became very good friends. I think it was my second semester at Delta and I was still taking ballet class with her. Now I was taking both the beginners ballet and the intermediate ballet. Around that time in the intermediate ballet, which was after the beginners, she had some of her students from her company there. So I was there along with the other students, trying my best to keep up with them. Which sometimes I failed with a capital F.

She looked at me and I believe she saw the potential or the drive that I had. She looked at me and said, "I want you to come to my class at my studio." I said, "Okay, what's the address?" She gave me her address where her studio was and I started going to her classes. So I started going to her morning classes at Delta and then after that I was going to her evening classes at her private residence at the studio.

Dorothy always teaches you everything starting from the basics and works up to the advanced. You always start from ground zero. The only difference in Delta is that it was a much slower pace. It was the same teachings that she taught in her studio, but it was much slower-paced because these students, yes some were interested in being ballet dancers, but others wanted to be dancers on Broadway or in theatre. So they needed to take ballet so they could add it to their repertoire. At the same time, the teachings were thought out methodically and very exact for these beginner students, such as myself. Now in her studio, it was the same teachings but of a more profound detail, a little bit faster pace.

By the end of the second semester at Delta, Dorothy told me "Oh, by the way, you're going to do *The Nutcracker* with us." I'm not fully trained classically.

I looked at her, "Are you sure I'm ready for it?"

"Oh, yes you'll be ready."

As a Mexican folk dancer myself, I started dancing as a child. So for me, when I started classical ballet, when she threw me in the fire doing *The Nutcracker*, it was like taking my first dance classes again. It was like reliving that moment. It was wonderful just to see the bodies in action moving around to the notes of Tchaikovsky in *The Nutcracker*. And here I am and she tells me "Oh, you're going to be Clara's father and you're going to be one of the Spanish dancers."

And I'm all "What?"

"You're going to do "Spanish chocolate.""

And mostly the second act of *The Nutcracker* is reserved for the guest artists that Dorothy brings from New York because that part of that act is very difficult to do. But for me as a first-timer, I was like, "Crap." I just remember I had no [finger] nails around that time because I was so nervous about it. But working with Dorothy throughout these years of my life has been a pleasure because you see this woman, and you see her mind going, you see everything, you see the full picture. When you are around someone who's been around their craft, for so many years, you can see everything. And by not even saying a word, you understand what they're saying. That's how I feel when I'm around her, I could just see it, I could envision as well as picture what she's wanting at that moment. So working with her is always a pleasure. My friendship with her, as you see I talk about her as this woman on this pedestal because she is to me. But at the same time, I've grown to love her and we have become like almost grandson and grandmother. So as well, I have this infinite affection and love for her as my grandmother. Every time I see her I tell her, "If you need something, or you feel alone, or you need me, I will drop everything and without hesitation, I will go to your house." And she knows that. So I have profound respect, love, and admiration for this woman.

So I was already in my 20s, I believe I was 21, already adult age. Dorothy was going to go to New York every summer to take her students to Joffrey to further their education in classical ballet. She asked, "Do you mind if you take care of my house during the summer for a month?"

I said, "Sure. I don't mind. I'll take care of it."

I remember I was taking care of her house for a month and her phone was ringing off the hook. It was several calls but I do not remember the names of these dancers. It was several calls from different dancers. "Oh, my name is so and so, I'm from this ballet in New York, is Dorothy there?"

Around that time, I would say, "I'm her nephew. I'm taking care of her house."

"Oh, can you please let her know? I'm wondering if she has Sugar Plum Fairy open still? I would like to be her Sugar Plum."

And there was another one calling to see if they could be the Cavalier for *The Nutcracker.* So I remember all these calls would swamp in because that's how known she is.

Another time I was house-sitting for her and I went to Lucky's which is a couple of blocks away from where she lives. I believe the security system alarm went off so when I came back, the police were there and they asked: "Do you live here?" I said "No, I don't live here, I'm house-sitting. My grandmother lives here and she's in New York."

They looked at me, "Who is your grandma?"

"Dorothy Percival, I can show you her office."

So I showed them the office, and the police were like, "This is an interesting house. Can we walk around and look at it?" "Sure, go for it." They asked, "Do you know the history of this house?" And I told them, "Well, this used to be the old Ranger Hall." They were in the living room and I said, "That used to be the stage."

So I'm walking around the house and I'm telling them the history because grandma Dorothy gave me the history about the house. So here I have three grown six foot two, six foot four

cops walking with me throughout the whole house. "This is a really neat house." they said and I said "Yeah, this is my grandmother's house."
"And she lives here by herself? She must be a strong woman."
"Oh, she is, believe me." I said.

Remember she owned her first dance company at the age of 15. From 15 till now she has not stopped. She is one of these people who does not like staying at home and sauntering about in the house, she doesn't like that. She likes to be active all the time.

She always wants a beautiful clean technique, but if you don't have that technique or step that she's wanting, she works on your strengths. My strength was my chaîné turns, I love to spin fast so she worked on my strength, and turning, and kicking, and jumping. There are some other strengths that I'm very poor at that she never used. But there were times where I needed to use them and she worked on them with me— she got me to improve and be better.
Across the country, she's known for her technique. I have seen her work with these marvelous dancers that she brings from New York. It's really interesting because she just gives them certain ballet steps to do, she tells a woman I want you to do battement frappé, up to his shoulder, she'll do all these hand motions to direct them from one place to another. It's like she's conducting a symphony with her hand movements and her arms are moving around.
I think with the more advanced dancers and dancers from New York she doesn't have to say much. I just see all these hands

moving around like if she was painting something. She tells them what to do and the dancers just look at her very attentively, keeping her focus on her. Then she just stands back and looks at them, and they start doing all these movements. She enjoys it. It's amazing to watch because it's on a whole different level. It's very interesting and almost entrancing to watch. Because of her, I had been a backup dancer for *Carmina Burana* which was another beautiful ballet. It was a long time ago, it was held by the Stockton Symphony and the Stockton Choir. They had wanted dancers so they called Dorothy to choreograph *Carmina Burana* so I was a backup dancer just in case. But I learned all my parts, like I did for another ballet La Traviata. I've been belly dancing and Mexican folk dancing for years prior to meeting Dorothy. I started dancing at the age of four and stopped for years until I picked it up again when I was 25. And she helped me in that area, very much so and she loves it. Since starting belly dancing again I've been doing it for 15 or 16 years plus. With the ballet background that I have from her, it has given me more stage presence, more elongating lines. Basically, I am very noticeable in belly dance. There are maybe about three or four more male dancers here in Northern California who are belly dancers. But I'm still very well known because of my posture, my long lines, and the ballet technique that Dorothy has instilled within me. She's always encouraged me. I always take her with me to my performances. I took her to six different belly dance performances, and they're big events in the Bay Area. More than 700 people go to these events. She just— she enjoys it, she's a true artist that appreciates every form of art, every form of how the body moves.

PATRICIA BLAND *was Dorothy's student from 2000 to 2011*
I had to have been about nine or 10 years old when I started
dancing with Dorothy so about 20 years ago.
I actually danced with Margret Smalling originally and Dorothy and Margret were lifetime friends. We got an invitation to
audition for *The Nutcracker* with Dorothy and it pretty much
started from there. My brother and I both danced, and we got
accepted. We got cast in *The Nutcracker*, and the relationship
just kind of grew from there. I danced for both studios for several years after that, and then I just went strictly to Dorothy.
Her teaching method was very, very strict but she got great results. You could really tell her passion that she had for teaching
and her love of ballet, she just wanted to pass that on to everybody. And she really shows that when she's teaching and the
technique was far beyond what I had ever known about. Way
better technique and better teaching method.
She was and is intense. She is amazing. To be able to work with
her was always an honor, I always felt very privileged to have
been able to study under her. Not only her but the people that
she brought in, like Amelia Gooden from Russia. She brought
him in several times as a master ballet class. It was just phenomenal. A once in a lifetime experience.
Dorothy was more than a ballet teacher to me, she's family.
After a long rehearsal or a long day of classes, we always went to
dinner afterward. That was pretty much an everyday thing for
us. We would talk about what we studied in class, or just life in
general. We always went to Lyons until they closed. There were
some things I didn't fully grasp something (maybe in class), and

that would give me the opportunity to sit down and really pick her brain because it was just me and her. She always explained things in a way that you can understand it, but sometimes it didn't always click.

So then she would try to do it in a different way— but a lot of times we would just sit down and talk about life and if there was a problem that I was dealing with, you know, as a teenager. Teenagers go through God knows what, she always had advice, and she'd always tell me, "I'm just an old lady. I'm going to give you my advice, you can take it or you can leave it or throw it out." or something like that. And 99% of the time, she was always right. Whether I took it or not, I've learned that, either way, she was right.

We've had great conversations. In class though, she was, like I said earlier, very strict. But she did it out of love. You had your ups and downs with her of course, but you knew at the end of the day, she was doing it to better you.

Any time I was turning, I couldn't turn to save my life. And she tried so hard, I still can't turn. And she would get frustrated too because she knew I was trying, but I just still never could. I could never turn as good as anybody else, I don't know just something about that. And that part was frustrating because she knew I was trying. She would get frustrated and she's loud. You know, she may not even be hollering at you but some-times it sounded like she was. So it didn't normally bother me. But when I would get so frustrated with myself, that really did bother me because I really thought she was yelling at me and she wasn't.

We were always in competition, we always wanted to be better than each other. That was a normal thing, if you really wanted it, you were always in competition with whoever was better at something than you were. You always strived and that was something Dorothy taught you. You always strive to be better than the next.

I did not actually compete, Dorothy wasn't doing too much competition stuff at the time. She did it a few times over the years but it really wasn't her thing– she put on a lot of shows. We would do out of town shows but we didn't do competitions. It was amazing, every year was different. I did *Nutcrackers* with her from the time I was probably 10 years old until, I think the last one I did I was probably 21. It was right before I moved back to Mississippi.

Every year was different and in my younger years when I first started it was definitely a learning process. Because I had never done such a big production so there was a lot to learn about how a big production is put on like that. It was a great learning experience, of course, and just the rush of putting on a show like that is amazing. There's a lot of work that goes into it, lots of hours of rehearsal. I can remember a time, especially when I got older, we'd be there till midnight rehearsing which we all loved.

Choreography was always different. Our venues would change. So you'd have to work with different stages. Most of the times we had a live orchestra, I can count on one hand where we didn't have a live orchestra. So having a live orchestra to me is like, a lot more exciting, because you never know what the tempo is gonna be, you've been rehearsing with a CD and it's

always the same. But then when you go into your dress rehearsals and stuff like that, it's always different. But our choreography
was always different, you know the people change, and then
you have open auditions. So you get these new people in, that
you've never worked with before. And some of them don't fully
understand that if you're in my way, I'm gonna run over you
kind of thing.

That was a lot of work too. I mean you got costumes, and she
basically did all of it. Pretty much by herself. I mean as originals
that were always there we helped her out, we would run rehearsals and help with the younger kids rehearsal and stuff. You
know, we would run those. It was a group effort, but she did put
everything together.

It was great if you were able to do that. You've earned Dorothy's
trust, and she was comfortable with your ability in teaching
and running rehearsals. So to be able to do that, to me, was just
an honor that she trusted me with that. We were able to run
the little kids rehearsals, and then there were times that we ran
our own rehearsals. So yeah, it was actually an honor because
like I said, if she allowed one of her students to run a rehearsal and help teach the younger kids, she definitely believed in
their ability.

I flew back a couple of times to be a guest artist.

And I tried [to do ballet here] in Mississippi, though.

Well, not where I live I mean. You got Ballet Memphis, up in
Tennessee, which is only about an hour from me. But it's still a
lot to have to go out there that late and then have to drive back
that late. I did find a small studio that I started teaching at, I
started taking lessons and then they were like, "We need you to

be a teacher." So I started teaching and then I had my son. After I had my son, they actually closed down about six months later. There's just nothing else here that was worth even trying. When I started teaching here, I would call her for advice on how to get it to click for a kid because that's something that you're always wanting. That moment of when you see that the child has actually gotten what you were teaching them. That's like the best feeling and that's why we teach. You don't get them every day, you may not get them in a month, but that one that you do get is just the best feeling.

She is family, my son has never actually met her, but he calls her Grandma Dutchy. He talks to her on the phone all the time. It literally just all stemmed from taking classes and somehow, we just had this click. She helped me out a lot, you know, growing up with different problems family-wise, really.

She was just always there to mentor me and she just became basically like a mother to me, or grandmother I guess. She's a big reason of who I am today. In class, you work your hardest to get where you want to be, you may not always get there, but at least you know you did your best to do it. And that poured over into life, everything that she taught in class, she taught you that you can use that in day-to-day life.

My dad died when I was 13 years old and she was there for that. She saw how much that hurt me, and she helped me work through that a lot. At one point in time, she even helped me find a counselor because I was really struggling. She went with me to the counselor. My mother and I never really got along, we get along better now since I've had my son, but back then we didn't. And then when I lost my dad, that just about killed me. So she really, really helped me through that. She took a big part in that. And then taking the things from class, it pours over into your everyday life, which meant basically "get your ass up off the ground and get moving." That was something that I use every day: don't just sit down, don't hang around and be lazy. I talk to her every week. I tell her what's going on here. If I'm having a problem, either at work or at home or with my son, I call her and ask what do I do? And it's always, "This is just my little old lady advice, you can take it or you can throw it out. But this is what I'm gonna say, you may not like it, but I'm gonna say it."

And again 99% of the time she's right, and I find out either the easy way or the hard way. I've learned though, do it the easy way. Just do what Dorothy says, it usually works out better. I can't think of a time where she wasn't pushing. She always strived for the best.

We pretty much were all friends. I mean, we were together every day for four to eight hours. So we were basically all one happy family, really. I mean, we had our ups and downs, I'm sure. Especially if we were partnering or something and it wasn't going well. One of us would probably get frustrated, but we always worked it out. I don't recall ever having any major differences with any of the other company members.

CHAPTER 23

The Nutcracker

ADRIAN JUNEZ

The Nutcracker is her baby. Her *Nutcracker* shows, as the people of San Joaquin County or the people who have known Dorothy have seen, they are beautiful. They're colorful, they're lively, they have characters. Dorothy, always from what I've seen, has her dancers become a character. She tells us ahead of time, months in advance, "This is how I want you, your character to develop, I want your character to develop this way or a sort of way that it develops, and it becomes second nature." It gives it that meat that you can bite in so the audience can see that we're not all these pretentious, snobby ballet dancers on stage, but we're more human. We can relate to the audience. Yes, we are artists and we're performing on stage but at the same time, we're being relatable to the audience. I've seen how Dorothy works her craft that way while mastering her technique.

It's stressful because it takes a lot of hands. A lot of parents have to move everything around from backdrops to props, lighting, and music. She is the director, and she's the artistic director, and the choreographer of our company. I'm just there as a stagehand

and as a dancer. So when she needed me to move things around I was there, when she needed me to sew something I was there. She was a trooper, a sergeant, a general– she moved forward all the time.

I would say maybe two months, three months before *The Nutcracker* she would be starting with the little kids, with the babies, with the little girls. I mean, she works her way from the children all the way up to the adults. All to make sure what she sees she likes and that it looks good from far away. If she doesn't like it, then she says no, I don't like this change and it gets changed.

It needed to be run that way, to tell the truth, so everything could be on time, so there's a flow.

And to *The Nutcracker* performances: there's always a flow for when everything comes on or the backdrop changes or the curtains open a certain moment, there's a flow to everything. It has to be mastered and maneuvered like a sergeant so the pace of the show could go on, and not seem to bore the audience. I don't want to say bore them to death but you have to keep them interested and wanting more. So, there's a certain pace to every-thing, how everything should be moving.

I was behind the stages when we needed to bring props and we needed to bring the backdrops and fix that tree that she has in the first act. We're in the battle between King Rat and the Nutcracker against a tree that is elongated and gets bigger and bigger. We needed to fix it, put it on stage and decorate it– and it's always with her. She seems cool and calm once we rehearse it with costuming, lighting, and props. Then she relaxes but before that she's looking at every single detail.

PATRICIA BLAND

He [Adrian] is a trip and a lot of fun. He does exaggerate; one time I was doing Russian (The Trepak character dance) in *The Nutcracker*. And the costumes that we had just weren't really working for what we were doing that year. It was actually me and him, we were doing a duet and that's one of my favorite parts of *The Nutcracker*. Dorothy pretty much cast me in Russian every year. But anyways, he was gonna make me a costume because he's big time into sewing. Just very artistic with that kind of stuff, very talented or so I thought. Well he got my measurements and everything. And I actually ended up having somebody else make my skirt for that because he didn't make the skirt. He ran out of time for that, he said but he was gonna make the top. He ended up going to Target and bought one and then tried to say that he made it. I'm like, "Dude, it's got a tag in it!" He actually is a very talented seamster but he just didn't do it. He's kind of a procrastinator too but he's a lot of fun to work with. He's a lot of fun to dance with, very light-hearted. He's just not somebody that you can stay mad at, you know what I mean? Adrian's probably been one of my best friends for over 20 years.

ADRIAN JUNEZ

There's no rest but it's a good because you accomplish something and you know that everybody liked it and they're anticipating for the next year to see it again.

Dorothy had set out from the beginning of her time in Stockton to establish a full-fledged professional ballet company in the city. Dorothy could see with the students that entered her classroom and studio every day that the potential was there to make something that could compete with The Sacramento Ballet and even The San Francisco Ballet. As mentioned by Melissa Esau, there were many organizations and boards working towards making Stockton a beacon of the San Joaquin Valley when it came to the arts. After all, the city was home to the famous landmark the Fox California Theater, which is now named the Bob Hope Theater. But the problem is that Stockton has a lot of problems when it comes to poverty and crime, so the arts are not exactly on the top of the list for the city. But I think that is why Dorothy gravitated to building something in Stockton so much, rather than go to somewhere like San Francisco. She came from a poor neighborhood during the Great Depression– I even remember being asked to hang up posters for her *Nutcracker* ballet as a teenager in some of the roughest neighborhoods in Stockton because she said, "Those are still my people."

Dorothy's frustrations and struggles were documented in a 2006 article from the *Stockton Record* titled "Ballet in Stockton a tough sell?" by Ian Hill. Hill documents how after 40 years of putting on her annual show of *The Nutcracker*, Dorothy had to cancel it after losing thousands of dollars on previous years' productions. This was followed up with her having to cancel a production of Dracula when only 72 tickets were sold. It really put into perspective the uphill battle that Dorothy was fighting in Stockton, not only with the city not giving the arts proper funding but just the people themselves. Accord-

ing to Hill, "Experts say the reason there's a definite ceiling on
the Stockton classical audience lies in the city's demographics.
Stockton does not have a high percentage of the types of people
who, research shows, patronize such events."
According to the U.S. Census Bureaus 2005 American Community Survey, Stockton is a diverse community where 53
percent of the residents are white, 37 percent are Hispanic and
23 percent are Asian. The median age is 29, per capita income
is $18,976 and 17 percent of residents have bachelor's de-
grees." (Hill).

The truth is, many of the people who populate Stockton just
aren't the kinds of people who flock to ballets or other kinds
of arts. At first, when researching this part of Dorothy's story, I
had thought maybe she, and the rest of the Stockton Arts Commission had misjudged their market but a couple of paragraphs
in Hill's article stuck out to me that made me feel otherwise.
The first one was a quote from Professor Carl Grodach:

Carl Grodach is an assistant professor in the School of Urban and Public Affairs at the University of Texas at Arling-
ton and has studied the role classical arts play in California
urban development. He said organizations need to consider their community's demographics if they want classical
performances to be successful.
"It's about knowing what's in your city and who's in your
city and targeting it that way," he said. (Hill)

The next quote that stuck out was from Ted Libbey:

Ted Libbey, author of The NPR Listener's Encyclopedia of Classical Music, said classical arts groups might expand their popularity among Latinos if they reach out and invite Latinos to serve on their boards of directors.

"You've got to find those people, and I'm convinced you can find them anywhere you have a large enough population," Libbey said. (Hill)

The problem comes from the fact that mainstream arts organizations are mostly run by, and geared towards white people and when you look back through Dorothy's long career, most of the people who put roadblocks up for her were white men. Not only that but the boards that Dorothy was on for the city were made up of white people with Dorothy being the only person of color there, being of Mexican and Native American descent from her mother.

Because of this, Dorothy was the only one who made an effort to reach out to all members of the community with ballet. You can see that with how diverse her ballet classes were. Dorothy was a one-woman army. It did not matter how much funding she got for her ballet company if she was the only one reaching out to all parts of Stockton's diverse population while the city and the rest of the arts commission ignored them. It was doomed to fail, unfortunately.

The following year, in 2007, a scathing article was written by reporter David Siders again in the *Stockton Record*. This article titled "Stockton says ballet bit city for $10,000" covers how the arts commission gave Dorothy a $10,000 grant to put on her *Nutcracker* show at the Bob Hope Theater. Since Dorothy had to cancel the show due to low ticket sales the commission wanted their money back, but Dorothy petitioned for her to be able to keep the money and use it for a smaller scale show in Lodi, Ca. with the same cast. But the commission argued that the money was for a show that was to be performed in Stockton. At the time, Dorothy was the head of the Professional Organization for Performing Arts (POPA), and had just had knee surgery. Siders interviewed Dorothy at her favorite spot, House of Shaw while she was having lunch. Of the interview Siders stated, "She called the situation a sad act, a 'pissing contest' in which the commission badly reacted, offending an artist who has for years devoted herself to Stockton."

With growing pressure from the city Dorothy had gotten frustrated and began trash talking the arts commission: very, very vocally. This caused arts commission boardwoman Donna Brown to step in– while she did not appreciate Dorothy's bad mouthing of the commission, she did have this to say about Dorothy in the article:

"'People in this county in the arts, particularly in ballet, don't get very far unless they're very pushy or aggressive and stand their ground,' Brown said this week. 'And Dorothy has gotten where she is by standing her ground'" (Siders).

This led Dorothy to make a proposal to the commission to use it for a smaller scale show but this time in Stockton.

CHAPTER 24

Crossing Paths With Dorothy

A few years later is where I cross paths with Dorothy– well sort of. My mother, Lisa, was looking to enroll my younger sister, Marta, in ballet lessons but she wanted somebody who you would say, "was on another level." As she was researching different ballet instructors she started hearing about a ballet instructor in Stockton, California with a passion for excellence. Mom began bringing Marta to ballet lessons with Dorothy five days a week and it became my sister's whole life. I was in high school at the time and would occasionally go with my mom to pick up/drop off my sister at practice when I didn't have any after school activities. I would only see the outside of her home studio that so many of Dorothy's former students spoke about. It was a corner house with an upstairs loft, it had a mysterious quality to it. The back was full of trees all wrapped up by a wooden fence. On the side of the fence there was a little path that led to a gate where you would enter the studio through the backyard. My mother and I would always sit in the car while we waited for my sister to finish with her lessons. For the first couple years of my sister doing ballet, I never saw Dorothy. I kind of built up an image in my head of who this woman could be and what she was like.

Eventually I asked my mom if I could go in and get my sister after she was done just so I could see the inside of this studio. I made the walk up to the gate that so many of her previous students have now told me about, walked along a small path through the perfectly landscaped backyard and onto the back porch. The porch had some wind chimes, plants, and a few places to sit– but what really caught my attention was the sitting area inside. I entered and it was just before the students came downstairs.

The room felt like something out of a movie. The walls were covered in dark rustic wood panels, there was a small writing desk nestled under the stairs covered in paperwork and a few wooden cabinets, all of which were antique. The walls had posters and pictures from Dorothy's previous shows, and I got a sense of her immense history with ballet.

Finally, the students came down and I got to finally see the five foot tall Dorothy in person at last. We introduced ourselves to each other quickly before I left. Eventually Marta began doing shows and this meant six grueling days a week of practice.

This goes back to what I was saying in the prologue; that seeing the finished product like a show doesn't really give you an idea of the amount of work and dedication that goes into it. I first realized this when seeing how Marta and her fellow students had to live and breathe ballet just like Dorothy in order to pull off a show like they did. During this time Dorothy began holding her annual Nutcracker shows again, this time at University of the Pacific. These were eventually followed up by productions of *Lon Po Po* and other ballets. Over the years, I got to briefly meet Tamara and Adrian as they both were involved in Dorothy's company, with Tamara being one of my sister's main teachers.

As I got into college, I began taking my sister to ballet classes more often as I found the waiting room in Dorothy's studio to be the perfect place to do my homework. I could hear from down in the waiting room the footsteps from the students and Dorothy shouting the same commands over and over. They had to do the same steps over and over again in order to get it right and during the shows I got a chance to observe Dorothy working behind the scenes. As many mentioned before, she ran the backstage of her shows like a drill sergeant because she had to. Costumes had to be organized, props had to be organized– if one thing went off schedule, it would have a domino effect on the rest of the show. It is no wonder Dorothy used to smoke cigarettes while working. Through these productions, Tamara was right there with Dorothy working to make these shows work. Despite the two of them having a rocky relationship and butting heads behind the scenes, they worked together to put on some truly beautiful shows. And from the outside looking in, you wouldn't suspect any of the problems the two were having behind the scenes.

The roadblocks that Dorothy has always faced did not stop in later years, unfortunately. Dorothy had been taken advantage of by some of the parents who wanted to get free lessons out of her, and to top it off, it still cost a ton of money to put on her shows. Which meant Dorothy had to start coming up with more ways to cover these expenses.

MARTALISA BENSON *was Dorothy's student from 2009 to 2019*

I started dancing at Bolshoi West when I was just four years old. Due to my young age, I was placed in Tamara's beginner class, as I wasn't yet old enough to be Dorothy's student. Although I don't remember much of Tamara's beginner class, I recall having a fun-filled time while learning the basic principles of dance. Right from the start I formed strong bonds with the other girls in my class, and I became very close with all of them. Although I haven't kept in touch with the other students, they hold a special place in my heart. We learned, laughed, and grew together, and created a bond that I will always cherish.

As the years went by, I progressed through the ballet classes, gradually gaining a deeper understanding of the art form. Dorothy played a huge role in my development as a dancer and as an individual. Under her guidance, I not only honed my dance skills but also learned essential life lessons and values like self-respect and respect for others. In my personal life, I struggled with shyness and found it challenging to be sociable and to verbalize my thoughts. However, dancing at Dorothy's company proved to be transformative. It helped me develop the social skills I needed to communicate and connect with those around me.

At the end of each class, Dorothy made it a point to hug each one of her students, taking the time to discuss our personal lives. Dorothy became like a grandmother figure to me. My maternal grandparents both passed away by the time I was 10, and my paternal grandparents were in a different state across the country. Dorothy helped to fill the void that I felt was empty. She was nurturing to all her students, but also firm in teaching us discipline and manners, both within and outside the studio. However, as Dorothy grew older, I noticed a shift in her focus. It seemed that she began prioritizing certain students, possibly due to her age and a desire to invest in those who were dedicated to pursuing a professional dancing career. This shift left many of us feeling left behind and disappointed. I, in particular, never received my coveted pointe shoes, a dream I had ever since I started dancing.

Tamara's classes differed from Dorothy's, not only in teaching style but also in her attitude toward her students. Toward the end, I found myself enjoying Tamara's classes more. She recognized our capabilities and pushed us to achieve our fullest potential. Unlike Dorothy, Tamara treated every student equally, not favoring any particular individual. There were occasions when Tamara would even argue with her mother advocating for students like me who were ready for pointe shoes. Dorothy, however, insisted on adhering to her own timeline.

In the last few years I spent at Bolshoi West, I witnessed many of my friends departing from the world of ballet. We were growing up, and our interests and priorities were changing. As a high school freshman, I experienced the sorrow of witnessing the closure of Bolshoi West due to financial difficulties. Each day after that brought a sense of emptiness, as something I loved so deeply was suddenly no longer a part of my life. Following the closure, I briefly danced at another ballet company in Modesto, California. Unfortunately, my journey was abruptly halted because of Covid-19 and my severe scoliosis.

In June 2020, I underwent surgery to address my scoliosis, and since then, I have been unable to dance. It is a profound sadness to realize that I was unable to achieve my dreams in ballet. However, I still learned so many valuable lessons and principles throughout my journey. I credit both Dorothy and Tamara for helping me understand the importance of pursuing my aspirations and overcoming obstacles. They instilled in me the resilience I need to continue pursuing my dreams.

CHAPTER 25

Loss of the Stockton Studio

In order to keep finances up for her shows, Dorothy had begun taking some bad advice from individuals at her church who convinced her that the best course would be to take money out of her houses. This turned out to be a big mistake, as her financial situation worsened, and with her still butting heads with the Stockton Arts Commission it came to the point that she had to sell her home studio in Stockton which was truly the end of an era for San Joaquin Ballet. Gone was that iconic waiting room and dance floor that so many students from all walks of life passed through.

I asked Dorothy why she lost the home studio in Stockton and she fired back with, "I didn't lose it, I sold it! I just got tired of the Stockton politics, they still can't get their head out of their butt. I would love to be able to tell the Mayor [Michael Tubbs at the time], the new one coming in, what I could do for Stockton if they just let me go in there and put a dance studio right near the old Fox theater. They're not smart enough. You know, what do they have? A bunch of crap. Nobody so far has had the background that I have to put into that town."

MELISSA ESAU

We used to have the Stockton Arts Commission, it was created by my husband's aunt, Mary Jacobs. And it was big, it just was so different back then, where the arts were literally flourishing in the area. The Arts Commission would give money to Dorothy and they just lost their way because people stopped wanting to participate. And then it became all this thing about the revitalization of sports. It just kind of went the other way and she's right, they didn't know a good thing when they had it and they just didn't have the right people to support it. They had other priorities. The opera Association kind of fell by the wayside too, and the Stockton Symphony is struggling and not just because of COVID.

Dorothy goes on to talk about Downtown Stockton and the potential that downtown Stockton has with it being linked to the San Joaquin/Delta river which can be taken all the way out to San Francisco Bay.

"And to see the yachts coming down that river. I could see the yachts coming in to see a good ballet and not just to have coffee with Spanos. That's the only thing they ever did, come down the river, hardly get off your yacht, have a cup of coffee or food, come back to the yacht and go back to San Francisco. Before I die, I'd like to have one more chance to make Stockton what it was when it was first discovered. To not even answer a telephone call, that's pathetic."

CHAPTER 26

The COVID-19 Pandemic

Dorothy has since attempted to establish Ballet San Joaquin in Stockton at a different studio space but unfortunately, the COVID-19 pandemic shut her business down with lawyers banging at her door for the rent owed on the space. But Dorothy's answer was always "if I can't work how am I supposed to pay you?" As she goes stir crazy in her house at 91 years old, constantly cleaning and dusting to stay busy, it has become clear that Dorothy isn't happy about how her career seems to be wrapping up.

"I'm really really really really, really unhappy that I can't finish my story because I want to leave something here that another Dorothy Percival can take advantage of. It's crap mostly, they're just making money and I never did it for money. That's a failure in my life. I've never failed at anything in my life, yet somebody or something is keeping me alive? Because I don't eat right, I don't drink, I don't sleep well. It's just this, there's no reason to live if that makes any sense? I'm not saying I should die or I'm going to kill myself. I'd never say that, but there is no reason.

Because otherwise, I sit here, I dust, I clean the same things over and over again." explained Dorothy.

"Retirement is not your thing?" I asked.

"No, there's nothing to retire from. Why would I retire? Right now, I was forced to retire and I'm going cuckoo. I think that's what kills people. Because when you get to be my age even your family begins to think you're stupid. They begin to treat you like you've lost your brain. So that makes me a little testy. So this isn't one of those places where the family gathers but friends do."

It became clear to me that Dorothy, after everything she'd done, all the people she met, all the things she had accomplished, was feeling like a lonely failure. I think this comes from the fact that Dorothy is a "hungry" individual, meaning she needs to always have something to go after, she needs a goal. And as artists, many of us often are hungry to accomplish something that proves we were alive, to leave our mark on the world. To leave some kind of a legacy, and to Dorothy, she hasn't been able to accomplish that.

But this is where I'm going to do something that so many people in her life have been so terrified to do: I'm going to disagree with Dorothy Percival. Dorothy does have a legacy, and that legacy is the hundreds of students that she has impacted at her studio. From the ones I've interviewed to the ones that turned me down, and the ones that I couldn't find; whether they like it or not, Dorothy has had a huge impact on shaping them into who they are today. Don't just take my word for it: hear it straight from them.

CHAPTER 27

Dorothy's Impact on Her Students

BETH MAIN

Most recently, I worked for HBO where I won an industry award and had the opportunity to give an acceptance speech. I only had three minutes but I think I took four. I spent a lot of time thinking about what I wanted to talk about. Here I am now. I was 60 years old at the time, had really reached a moment in my executive career that was hard-won and so satisfying. And here, I had the opportunity to speak at a conference, I was given complete freedom to do what I wanted with the time. I went through many drafts, thinking three minutes, what do I want to focus on? There's so much I can talk about. I kept throwing out version after version, and I kept coming back to Dorothy and the experience I had, essentially growing up with her. I decided that's what I wanted to talk about because it's in retrospect it's so clear to me now in ways that never was before, that my ballet training with Dorothy are inextricably connected and so foundational, and what I learned from her as a result of that extraordinary experience has benefited me all my life.

No matter what I've done, including my success as a corporate executive for HBO, there's no question that one led to the other.

I started at Dominican College of San Rafael because my mom had gone there and because it was tied to the Marin Civic Ballet School which is a very good school. I thought here's what I'll do, I'll please Dad and go to college but I'll stay in shape. I'll take classes every day at the Marin Civic and then I'll go back to dancing. That was my original thought, but you can't do that if you want to excel at something whether you're a sculptor, a painter, musician, or a writer. You can't do it half-assed, you're either going to do it and create something noble out of it or you're going to dabble. You can't go to college and be a professional ballet dancer at the level that I wanted to be at, the level that Dorothy trained me for.

But I came to peace with it, as over the course of years I came to love university life. I did take classes every day at the Marin Civic Ballet School for about a year, but then as the months and years went on, I found that I love to eat. I loved to study, write, and do other things. But I did not keep in touch with Dorothy. I went from one extreme to the other because I was so certain that I had broken her heart. She's tough, she could handle it, but I didn't give her that chance until much later. So now it's 1989, I graduated from UC Santa Barbara. That's where I ended up and you know when you graduate from college you're still young enough to get in shape and so I did. When I graduated I had no idea what I wanted to do. I studied English literature, and I just had clue zero so I thought, "Well, what do I know how to do? Nothing, except I can write well and I can dance or used to be able to dance so I got back in shape.

I auditioned for the Santa Barbara Ballet Theatre and I got in the core. So it's fall 1980, I'm in the core de ballet of the Santa Barbara Ballet Theatre, which doesn't exist anymore. And I danced there for a couple of years; it was my first job. It was a professional job because I got paid for it. But it was a regional company and the regional companies don't achieve the same levels of excellence that the big guys do. But it didn't matter; it was so satisfying, it was so wonderful that I got to perform. I was reminded that my world had become bigger. And with ballet, you have to want it and only it or you're not going to make it. And I didn't; it wasn't a need, it was a delight. But if it's not a need you can't withstand the rigors.

So I quit, quit in 1982 and I haven't even taken a ballet class since then. So I tried a lot of different things. I wrote a travel guidebook, I worked in cable television, worked in Silicon Valley. I studied to be a sign language interpreter for the deaf, I did a lot of different things. But what I learned with Dorothy really informed my value system. Perseverance through pain, whether it's physical or emotional, poise under stress, teamwork. When you're one in a line of swans, you have to give a damn about what your neighbors are doing so you can be on the same count and music with your head and your arm and your hands, etc. You have to be aware of others. It's not about you as a single contributor unless you have a solo. It's about being part of the team and what you can do together.

I learned to be a good coach from Dorothy, and I coached my staff in a similar fashion. When they'd come in with wringing of hands or bad behavior, especially those who would get pissed off about something but not find a productive way to express that anger; I held on and drew from my experience with Dorothy and it made me a good manager. I helped people see what gifts they had that they didn't see because they were young or they were immature. And that takes time for all of us. And I give that all to Dorothy. I've told all this to Dorothy in one way or another, she is such a gift. It comes at a price but all good things do.

Dorothy is very hyper-focused. I mean, when she was here in New York, the way she talked to the waiters. Like, whoa, girl. He's here to help you have a pleasant experience. You're not here to teach him how to be a better waiter. Those great gifts came at a price and I think that many of us benefited in ways that few did not. And that makes me sad too because Dorothy gave us so much.

KIMBERLI CAMPBELL

I think my particular personality has been to try to be less like that. Obviously my lifestyle choices were completely different, almost in opposition. I'm a very traditional mother, very traditional wife. I think maybe not oppositional because that's kind of defiant, but for whatever reasons, I tried to keep the peace a lot because sometimes artistic people can be pretty volatile. That's what I was thinking about today with my father, he was sort of a steady guy under the roof with a traditional job and not really climbing any sort of business ladder up to the CEO. He didn't really aspire to do that— he would just cook dinner every night and we would wait for my mom to come downstairs or to say goodbye to her last students. To come in and eat things like that. I'm almost counter to all of that. Sometimes I'd like to teach my husband a few things about having less of a giving wife, but it's what I've chosen to do.

I kind of took myself away from that whole world when I got married and started having kids. I did teach for her the first several years after I had my first couple of kids. She's supported a couple of my small dance studios. She always wanted us to sort of, not necessarily follow in her footsteps, but she always said, "If you can dance or teach dance you'll always have something you can do to make money." That was kind of the philosophy, and there were a couple of times I did teach dance in one town and she subsidized a school when I first moved to my current location because she encouraged me to start a studio there.

But then I started having kids and I realized that that world is totally counter to running a home because the hours are off. And that's how I grew up, my mother would go to work after school because that's when you teach everybody so we would come home and you know, wait till she was done eight or nine o'clock at night. So it's kind of a counter thing. So I quit doing all of that- and my daughter's, most of them, took dance for a little bit here and there. But it was the same sort of scenario of a mother whose a dance teacher and then a grandmother whose a dance teacher. I decided I didn't really want to do that.

TAMARA WAGNER

I just have a little easier going attitude but then again I'm a child of the 60s. And we have different personalities in the sense that I am a little, probably a lot more true tuned in to what's going on with the kids emotionally because I can't help but notice it. I just see it and I sense it and that's just the way I am. Whereas she's [Dorothy] not, or she doesn't really give a fruit about that. Because what's important is her reputation and how good the students would show her to be. I've never had that kind of drive or as strong of a drive. I mean for instance if we have some kids that were training and they're just kind of not getting it, they're not doing real well, they're not working real hard. She would have a conniption about, "Well, they take from me, and I don't want them going out there and dancing like they've had bad training." And I didn't really care about that. But it wasn't my reputation because I never had a reputation as an instructor. I would just do the best I could, and if it turned out pretty good, well, then good for me.

Anytime that you can do something that's difficult and you manage to achieve it, that's a big deal. So anytime that happened it was an important moment and that's what kept me going. Because I worked hard and because I had ability, there were successes. But success at the toll of emotional issues. That's one of the things about dance— that it's constant little achievements. And so all of those are pretty important.

ELIZABETH ARCHER
She [Dorothy] influenced me greatly— that experience of being in and part of a ballet company led to me forming my own youth dance company in Truckee, California. It was run as a nonprofit founded in 2002, and we've just done amazing things. So that legacy that she established in my life provided a lot of guidance.

It's affected me in a lot of ways; I went on to be a registered dental assistant and work in orthodontics for 16 years, which is very exacting work. The way I process a lot of these things in my life and the way my brain works is I'm constantly choreographing, even though I'm not dancing. I'm choreographing my surroundings with those artistic and creative ways to live my life. Based on those principles and values of commitment, honesty, and integrity. Those are really important values to me, and I think a lot of that I learned through my commitment to dance, and through Dorothy's values as well.

If you come into a studio you're supported— your fellow dancers have your back. You can go there and you can cry, or you can laugh or you can rely on each other as partners. That's a powerful thing, especially when you're a young team. That's something that I tried really hard and accomplished in my own studio. I hear that over and over from my own students, "InnerRhythms is like being home." And that was something that was important to pass on from Dorothy, because you spend so much time there it better be like home.

It's interesting, Dorothy made a lot of sacrifices in her own family because she spent so much time with everyone else's family meaning all her young dancers over the years. I liken it to, again, my own experience with my own dance school. I had a lot of daughters and sons. You care about each and every one of them. And sometimes your own children and your own husband take a backseat. Being so convicted to your passion and your vision. Feeling like you're making a difference in your community, in other people's lives, doing things for other people before you do for yourself. I come from a place of not being an ego person, I just want to do good for other people.

That's my driving force and I think that I got that from Dorothy and her studio.

It was really an amazing thing to strive for because we wanted to be in that top tier especially from that creative and technical perspective. So it was just a really, really fine memory and a really, just a really great experience. Part of her [Dorothy's] legacy is that I wanted to share this and extend this to my own company. Not only training but my dancers have had the opportunity to work with world class dancers, world class choreographers, and gone on to world class companies. Dorothy is the seed that planted that.

The personal relationship that I had with her, I still have dreams about coming to the studio and walking up those stairs. Dancing there was just my favorite thing, learning choreography and working so hard to make it beautiful. Giving honor to the piece through that hard work— there's just so much to it, it's not any one thing that I can identify. I think it's just that the whole result of the legacy is my favorite thing, the effect. I am who I am today because of my experience and my relationship with her [Dorothy] and think about it all the time.

I just really want to give honor, respect, love, and gratitude. I'm just so filled with gratitude that I was blessed enough to have this time with her [Dorothy]. I should say I can't think of anything else that affected me so deeply in my life and I'm honored that I was invited to participate in the book as well.

MARCIA HENDRICKS

I had a real awakening when I had an internship at Oakland Children's Hospital, which was pretty intense. By then I was engaged to my now husband and we had talked of having a family and it dawned on me; I can't work with disabled kids all day and come home and treat my own kids normally. I will forever fear that what has happened to these other kids would happen to my own. And my other experiences had been in just straight outpatient orthopedic settings for my internships. So in my first job out of grad school I went that route and just loved it. And quite honestly, most people that have back injuries, neck injuries, any extremity injuries, you have to have a strong core in order to recover, your posture has to be good. It helps being able to really observe and be sharp with people's presentations or movements. My observation skills were really good, being able to visualize from knowing and understanding the training and dance, it all fit. I did that for many, many years. I just have recently retired just close to my 61st birthday and had a career of like 37 years and I have to say I have Dorothy to thank for having pointed me that way.

I portrayed myself as kind of being late to the party and training. But I love dance to this day and I kept on pursuing classes. I was very fortunate in the area that I live in to have quality studios with adult classes. I was taking pretty intense classes up until I was in my early 50s. My hips aren't so happy with that anymore, but I still support ballet. My daughter had a really enriching youth ballet experience as well.

In fact, that's a fun story because my daughter was trained at the School of American Ballet for four summers. It was the second summer we were there. I was there with another mom whose son was trained at ABT who had come up through Joffrey. And when this other woman was sharing the story about how she knew me and our backgrounds in dance, I think she had mentioned that I had danced in Stockton, and with Dorothy Percival. Then she was like, "Oh my God, do you know that Dorothy is in New York City right now?" Quite honestly I didn't keep in touch that much but that's how I learned that Dorothy would take her students to the Joffrey in the summer, and she would stay in Rico Costa's apartment.

The person was like, "Oh, here's her phone number!" so I just reached out and called Dorothy and said, "You won't believe this but here I am in New York City with my daughter, do you want to do lunch?" So we got together and had lunch and I introduced her to my friend and her son. Her son is Garrett Anderson, who has had quite a dance career with being a soloist in the San Francisco Ballet as well as Belgium, Ballet of Flanders, and Hubbard Street [Dance Chicago]. Now he's the director of Ballet Idaho. So that was fun to have lunch with Dorothy in New York City and that would have been in the late 1990s. Because my daughter graduated from high school in 2000. Yeah, late 90s.

About two years ago someone organized a reunion and she wanted to host it in her house. I was just blown away to see her. She's the same age as my mother and my mother is in assisted living and needs to walk with a four wheeled walker and has different health situations. When I saw Dorothy at that point she was clearly living independently, walking independently, loved her little dog. Her house was like a museum with wonderful gifts and posters from people. When she showed me the downstairs basement and then all of the costumes that have never been owned. I was like this is such a treasure. I was just blown away and that was a real rich evening to reconnect with others that I danced within. As I said, I always was kind of more of a wallflower. But it was very nice because people connect and they understand— it is just a very loving group.

My senior year I think that was when I got casted in *Bags* which was a Vesak piece. That was quite an experience to do that. When I went to UC Santa Barbara, I think it was my freshman year there, the regional ballet festival was hosted in Santa Barbara. So I was able to get tickets to see the different night performances and I think that was the night where Terry Pago's piece was first. It was the first time I saw him as a choreographer, which was really exciting.

The following year they were in San Jose and I was able to get there to see. They just kept soaring through the ranks of really performing awesome stuff, all the way around. After I left for college was when they started to do the big *Nutcracker* productions that were performed at the Delta theater. There was no *Nutcracker* in my time, that was after me.

I think you need to go all in. Dedication and trying to do your best to get it right. You got to get noticed so you got to be front and center. They're not gonna notice you if you hang out in the back of the class and you should thank your teachers for corrections, rather than feel bad. Because if they're not correcting you, they are not looking at you or they don't care. They don't think you're going to get any better. There was a lot of that respect being passed along from the ages.

A little side note I have to share was always the fun fond memories of jazz classes that were on Friday night. We just got to let our hair down and just be ourselves. And I think Dorothy loved doing it just as much with us.

MELISSA ESAU

The bottom line is, I think, trying to be the best that you can be at everything, and that can be a curse or it can be a blessing. You can kill yourself and make yourself crazy trying to be the best at everything. If you were to talk to my husband he would tell you, "Yeah, she tried to be super mom." And I think I pride myself in really being able to multitask really well. Like she [Dorothy] said, "If you settle for mediocrity, that's all you're gonna ever get." I think that particular thing about always trying to be the best, and I don't mean that in a snooty way or anything, it's just trying to always do what's right and do it correctly. Be a problem solver, not a problem creator in your job. Having the discipline to work through a problem and not be a whiner, or a complainer. You just sucked it up, did what you needed to do and move forward. Somebody else had asked me this a while ago and I said "You learned the art form of ballet, you did. But the art form of ballet comes from the discipline that it takes in order to do it correctly."

One of the things that I remember when we were at a gala performance and there were seven girls and we were in these beautiful costumes. It was a gorgeous ballet, it was really lovely-it was like a 20 minute ballet. And I remember people coming up to us after saying, "Oh my gosh, you guys were so beautiful, you have the most beautiful feet." Because Dorothy was always about using your feet and it wasn't so much about executing the step correctly, even though she wanted you to, it was about transitioning from one step to another. Which is really creating that art form of making ballet beautiful. So while you've got that you also got the discipline of making it the best that you can be. The artistry came after the discipline. You can't have the artistry unless you know how to execute everything correctly.

She was a taskmaster and like I said, sometimes it was hard. It was like, just shoot me now because I'm never gonna get this. But you go home and you think about it, and then you're like, "Okay, I can I come back tomorrow, and I do it again." And that was the thing, we kept coming back and doing it again. So we obviously loved it. And then there's the challenge of "I'm not going to give into this, I'm not going to give up, I'm going to keep pushing through." And that's part of that training. You either get on the bandwagon or get off, and most of us stayed.

She [Dorothy] understood that perseverance because she had to persevere through her life to get what she wanted. I don't know if she's told you the story about how she started out, but I mean who does that, in that era? That's how bad she wanted it— so she literally instilled that perseverance and that drive onto us. I don't know if it was intentional or just kind of manifested itself with everything. But she worked hard to get where she wanted to. Like I said, back in the day, she was a force to be reckoned with. Everybody knew who Dorothy Percival was, and everybody knew that Dorothy Percival ran an amazing company. She worked hard to keep it up there with the level of the Stockton Civic Theater, the opera, and the symphony. Those were the four big art groups in this town; and she had a great board of directors, people donated money, and we had fund-raisers. It was a big deal.

But she worked really hard, blood, sweat, and tears to get what she wanted like when she wanted to utilize the Stockton Junior High auditorium where we used to have our concerts. She went to the city at one point said, "Hey, why not let me house my company there? I will keep it up. There'll be life, there'll be people coming and going." And the city said, "Yeah, you can use it, but you gotta clean it up." And she did, she cleaned it all up and got it functioning so that she could house her dance studio. She would have her dance studio at Stockton Junior High so that you could rehearse downstairs on the stage but you had two ginormous studios upstairs— and it was great. But you know, she went after that. She just was ballsy and just said, "Let me do this. Let me have this." and they said "Sure." She was a mover and a shaker.

Even at 90 years old, God bless her. She could still get her leg up as high as she could when she was 40. I told her the last time I saw her, which was at Christmas time. She has all of these videos and recordings of the company that I believe are on reel to reel. I said to her "You know, you should really take these and have them put on like DVDs so you could watch them again." I would love for her to do that not just because it's a super specific part of Stockton history that should be maintained because once it's gone it isn't there any more. And because the arts are struggling not just in Stockton, but all over. It would be great to have that legacy so that after she's gone, people can go back and look at that and go, "Wow, look what we had back in the 60s, 70s, and 80s in that unit."

She used to go out all the time. She used to go to House of Shaw over on Pacific Avenue, I don't know if she goes there anymore. That was her hangout.

Oh, yeah and Jim was great. Because you'd come downstairs and you'd be like, "Oh my god, what's he cooking? It smells so good." And you couldn't eat because you had to be rail thin. So it was hard to come downstairs and you'd smell all this good food coming up from the staircase.

When I saw that was being sold I was like, "Oh, that's a piece of my life." I lived there for 10 years and I have great memories I used to watch *Dance Moms*. I thought these women would have to be getting a lot of money to put up with that crap. Because Dorothy was tough but she was not evil towards each of us like that and pitting us against each other. She never did that, she only was about what's in yourself.

TERRY PAGO

I really never had a work ethic until I met Dorothy, I really never had a job actually. But through her work ethic, I had a better work ethic. I also learned from her if I wanted something I would get it no matter what. I don't know if that's a good thing or a bad thing. Because she would try to get to the target in a very polite, authentic way. If that wasn't possible she would go by other means to reach her target. And I have a little bit of that, I don't know if it's a good thing or a bad thing, personally. I use the word target, but it was a goal from performances to business ventures. If she could achieve something artistically and she knew what it was she would go for it and 99% of the time she got it and achieved the goal.

No, because she had already gone through those steps of refining who she was, or who she became. I had no idea until she told me, but she did tell me a story about the depression of her mother where they had to eat rice and beans a lot. So that was the first time I'd ever heard of somebody having to have rice and beans every night for dinner so I didn't forget that.

All in all, I think that Dorothy Percival did really good there. There have been a lot of hurt feelings going around. This is a terrible thing to say but all of the dancers have had the wounds of Dorothy Percival, some of them get over it and some of them don't. I, on my side, was so happy she took me in so I was happy to take a beating every once in a while, but not too much. I will say one thing, even though Dorothy had been really mean. She really wanted the best when push came to shove for everyone. It was a place of ego to get the best out of you. Getting something right was a goal; a particular movement was the goal for her to get right. She would try to artfully get it out of you. If you didn't respond to that she got it out of you and all means necessary and sometimes people left with hurt feelings.

It had been years. Once we all finally left we grew up and we have lives of our own. But the good thing about it is that there was always a respect for Dorothy Percival, no matter how much you liked her or hated her. You really couldn't hate somebody who aspired to be excellent.

ADRIAN JUNEZ

How to walk, how to carry your posture, how to stand. I mean the mark that Dorothy has left to me is that ballet was already within me. The way you carry yourself, the confidence because ballet dancers, we are confident, we are shown to be confident and to be confident.

Being in this small world of ballet you have to be confident in the art you do, because it's a beautiful art form. So within the ballet world and out, you're taught to be this competent individual, and it gives you strength and courage. And Dorothy has shown me how to be more confident within myself. I wasn't confident. As a young individual, as an 18 year old, I wasn't. Dorothy taught me how to be more confident, how to look up to people, how to look at them eye to eye when being spoken to. I can tell you this much when somebody yelled at me, I always look down. I always look down, like when a parent is scolding you and you look down, because you don't want to look at their look. You're like, "Oh crap, I did something wrong." That's the way I was before I met Dorothy. When someone yelled at me, I looked down. And she taught me no, carry yourself, look up, look at them eye to eye, show them that you're equal and that you're strong. She showed me that. And that's how I've been looking at the world, eye to eye. And that's the impact that she's left on me.

CHAPTER 28

Dorothy on the art of teaching ballet

"I don't have a lot of respect for the heads of the companies. They're good at their job which is business— I don't think they respect the art or the artists as much as they should. Because there are a lot of artists that are there because they're as crazy as I am, the passion. And to be treated as though you are stupid if you make a mistake, it's the passion, otherwise, why would they be there? Some of them also feel challenged if you're better than they are or know what you're doing. Each dancer may be an artist but unless you're having the court ballet [ballet de cour] where they all have to look exactly alike.

"But when you're a soloist, they're usually a soloist because they couldn't do anything else but live in the music. That's my opinion, there are some who think 'It needs to be only this way because that arm swings this way.' Well, the artist may be able to do it differently and still get over to the audience more so than the director. There are many, many directors that are terrific but you'll notice that they will let the artists work, and then they might discuss it instead of saying no, no, no, that's not right. If you chose that person to do that piece of work, and you chose them because they're an artist hopefully, not because they're good in bed hopefully, then listen to them."

I then asked Dorothy if she had experienced any of that kind of treatment during her career.

"All the time, I'm expected to kiss ass every time I turn around, even now. I don't try to interfere with your work, I don't know what your work is but I do know mine's good. And I do know I can get you where you want to go if you listen. Because there are just certain amounts of very, very fine little minute things that people don't even think about. They just do the steps, do the steps. That's why your core work is called core work, they're doing the steps and they do them very well. But as far as being the artist that's keeping the show up: because you usually don't go to a ballet or a show for the core work, you do it because the artist on top has got something going."

Dorothy then turned to me.

"You as an artist with your work, when people put things on paper they could put down in several different ways but when you do it one certain way you go 'Oh my.' One way might say 'The dog ran over the cat' or 'The dog, ran over the cat.' The companies and sometimes the directors, because they're trying to make a living they have to do what the board wants. And because of that you'll start to hear things like the dancers in the dressing room talking about these people behind their back."

Dorothy explained how if you're going to hire an artist, you need to let them create because as she puts it "An artist can't help it, they can't help being an artist. It's very difficult for me to put this into words because often I'm not allowed to talk like this because people don't understand what I'm talking about. It sounds like a bunch of gibberish to them unless you're talking to another artist. And I couldn't live without the arts, from the time I was born evidently. It's not me it's…" Dorothy pointed up, referring to the Man Upstairs. "…if you believe in anything, and sometimes I wonder why he did it. It interests me enough because I don't take much credit for a lot of stuff but my name itself, and once in a while I think about how dumb that sounds, but my name itself means gift of God." Dorothy chuckled. "And I cuss, and I carry on, but I'm human, and I know where I come from. And don't tell me that, that church is right and that one is wrong, please. That one is right." Dorothy pointed up again. "And I'm really not sure it's just one. And when somebody says they don't know what they want to do, I tell them to sit there real quiet and think about what is the thing that you really like to do, or really love that you're already doing. I think that's what he did, otherwise, why would I, born in Tracy, California, among poor people, want to be a ballerina? And there is so much more that I want to do, there is so much that I have forgotten that I've done, and I don't want to dwell on the past, but I want to take some things from the past and put them here…" Dorothy points to her head. "…and listen. And when young people like yourself say I'm not really happy with this job, well then do what the hell you were made to do!"

EPILOGUE

After three years I can finally see the encore of Dorothy's story. I still have this feeling that there are more students I need to speak with, students from her college courses, from my sister's classes, and from so many other time periods. But I have to come to accept that not everyone wants to share their story or pick up the phone.

I remember speaking to my friend Gerry Henderson, a retired Stockton librarian, while I was writing this book. He explained that even though he had never met her, Dorothy was known as THE Ballet in Stockton— to me it really showed how much of an impact Dorothy had on the area.

During the COVID-19 pandemic, Dorothy was forced to close down a new ballet studio that she had just opened up. This is not the way she was intending on spending her later years, as she describes going absolutely stir-crazy at her home.

As of 2023, she spends her days taking care of her multiple cats and dogs and keeping her extravagant home clean. Tamara, Kimberli, and Adrian visit regularly— Dorothy even flew back to Mississippi to be a part of Patricia's wedding. Unfortunately, she says regularly that she is not as close as she wishes with many grandchildren or nieces and nephews, nor do they seem to take any interest in her life.

But Dorothy still wishes that she could be teaching ballet in some form, which is understandable considering how much of her life has revolved around it. But excluding how things had ended with her studio, Dorothy has no regrets about her career or her life. She stands by every decision in all her stubbornness, though she still thinks about what could have been in terms of introducing a professional ballet company to the downtown area.

I look back at the journey writing this book has taken me on: the stress, the doubt, and all the times I wanted to quit. It is something that I know that I was clearly not ready for when I started it. Sometimes I think back and wonder if this book would have been in better hands if someone else wrote it rather than a neurotic, overly stressed, and inexperienced writer like myself. As I sat down and wrote the final chapters I could not help but feel that I could have done things differently or found more students. I think what lent to all these feelings was Dorothy's words ringing in my head. Her constant strive for perfectionism made me wonder if this book would live up to her. But her goal of inspiring others with her story of coming from nothing and building such an amazing life is what helped me see this project through.

During one of my last visits to Dorothy's grandiose house, she shared a quote with me by the late actor and comedian Milton Berle that I think perfectly sums up Dorothy: "I'd rather be a could-be if I cannot be an are; because a could-be is a maybe who is reaching for a star. I'd rather be a has-been than a might-have-been, by far; for a might-have-been has never been, but a has-been was once an are."

CAST
Dorothy "The Bitch" Percival
Beth Archer
Marcia Hendricks
Melissa Esau
Terry Pago
Adrian Junez
Beth Main
Tamara Wagner
Kimberli Campbell
Patricia Bland
Cheryll Kerr
Martalisa Benson

SPECIAL THANKS
Martalisa Benson, editor
Sandy Nguyen, editor
May-lee Chai
Mom and Dad

AUTHOR'S NOTE

This is my first book and it has been one of the hardest, and most stressful ordeals of my life. I had no idea what I was getting into when I reluctantly took on the task that my mother signed me up for. Many things happened while writing this book, a global pandemic, getting dumped by my longtime girlfriend, graduating college, getting my first full-time job, and losing my first full-time job.

My first real job was as a news reporter for my hometown newspaper, *The Calaveras Enterprise* and part of me wishes that this project came to me while I was well into that job because I felt I had a better grasp of non-fiction writing.

Now that this project is done I'm happy to start working on other writing projects, I'm thinking maybe a Lovecraftian horror graphic novel or a sci-fi story based in my hometown. Maybe I'll run some of these ideas by Dorothy during our next visit and see what she thinks.